SO-AAN-863

THE COMPLETE GUIDE TO

Business Agreements

Ted Nicholas

Enterprise · Dearborn
a division of Dearborn Publishing Group, Inc.

While a great deal of care has been taken to provide accurate and current information, the ideas, suggestions, general principles and conclusions presented in this book are subject to local, state and federal laws and regulations, court cases and any revisions of same. The reader is thus urged to consult legal counsel regarding any points of law—this publication should not be used as a substitute for competent legal advice.

© 1992 by Dearborn Financial Publishing, Inc.

Published by Enterprise • Dearborn,
a division of Dearborn Publishing Group, Inc.

All rights reserved. The text of this publication, or any part thereof, may not be reproduced in any manner whatsoever without written permission from the publisher.

Printed in the United States of America

92 93 94 10 9 8 7 6 5 4 3 2 1

Library of Congress Cataloging-in-Publication Data

Nicholas, Ted, 1934–
    The complete guide to business agreements / by Ted Nicholas.
        p.   cm.
    Includes index.
    ISBN 0-79310-489-0
    1. Commercial documents—United States—Forms. 2. Contracts—
United States—Forms. I. Title.
KF886.N53 1992
346.73´07´0269—dc20
[347.30670269]
                                                           92-18603
                                                              CIP

Books by Ted Nicholas

The Complete Book of Corporate Forms

The Complete Guide to Business Agreements

The Complete Guide to Consulting Success (coauthor, Howard Shenson)

The Executive's Business Letter Book

43 Proven Ways To Raise Capital for Your Small Business

The Golden Mailbox: How To Get Rich Direct Marketing Your Product

How To Form Your Own Corporation Without a Lawyer for under $75.00

How To Get a Top Job in Tough Times (coauthor, Bethany Waller)

How To Get Your Own Trademark

Secrets of Entrepreneurial Leadership: Building Top Performance Through Trust and Teamwork

Contents

Chapter 3: Setting Up Your Credit and Collection Program   59

Forms

Chapter 4: Leasing Commercial Space   97

Forms

Chapter 5: The Employment Relationship   123

Forms

Forms

How To Use Your Book

How This Book Is Designed for You

The Complete Guide to Business Agreements was drafted with the thoughts of the small to moderate-sized business in mind. The forms we've prepared for you cover commonplace business arrangements for which you ordinarily may be accustomed to paying professionals to prepare. Now, you have these forms at your fingertips.

When preparing these forms, we planned to serve you in many ways:

Preventing Disputes

If you've written an agreement that spells out each person's rights, you are in the best possible position to prevent later misunderstandings caused by different recollections of just what the agreement included.

Avoiding Lawsuits

By documenting an agreement, you not only avoid disputes based on faulty memories, but you force the other party to recognize what the agreement really provides. More so than any other preventative device, this should act to stop a person who no longer likes an agreement from suing. The written agreement, he or she realizes, will keep him or her from winning any challenge that he or she would mount if it is based on terms other than those in the agreement.

Eliminating Legal Fees

The forms in this book can be used without paying your lawyer to pull a standard form from his or her files and then charging you to fill in the blanks. More diligent lawyers will customize standard forms for their clients' circumstances. Depending on your needs, you may wish to have your lawyer review these forms. However, every form in this book has been reviewed by a lawyer to ensure that it is accurate and enforceable. If you are accustomed to having your lawyer regularly prepare standard agreements for your business, *The Complete Guide to Business Agreements* can save you thousands upon thousands of dollars every year.

Ensuring Performance

We've all met a person who enters into an agreement that he or she later regrets. If the agreement is not in writing, that person can easily walk away from his or her obligation to you. If the agreement is in writing, the other party knows that if he or she does not live up to the agreed-to promise, you can sue for damages. This, in turn, makes it more likely that he or she will make good on the contract's requirements.

Increasing Your Company's Efficiency

Because the forms in this book can be duplicated and used simply by filling in the blanks, you do not have to waste time and money going through the mechanical process of typing and preparing a form every time you need it.

Improving Accuracy

Again, because you can duplicate these forms on your office copying machine, you avoid the possibility of a typing error that could prove costly—remember, all you have to do is fill in the blanks.

Complying with State Laws

Many contracts must be in writing if they are to be enforceable; other contracts must follow a specific format if they are to be effective. Because the forms in this book satisfy these requirements, you can be assured that your written agreements will protect you. You may want to have an attorney review a contract to ensure that it complies with state laws.

Increasing Profits and Company Performance

By using standard forms for various business transactions, you ensure that your employees do not offer terms other than those you set as company policy.

This protects your company against poor pricing and bad debts, as it eases your collection efforts.

Avoiding Tax Difficulties

By formalizing your business agreements, you provide proof of any deductions or write-offs you take on your tax returns. Furthermore, we even provide a form that anticipates unfavorable tax treatment and puts that burden on others instead of on your business.

Using Forms You Can Understand

The forms in this book are not only valid and binding, but they are written in simple, straightforward language that you will understand with ease. You know, therefore, that you will not make a mistake because you did not understand what the agreement asked for with respect to any provision.

Working with Your Book

Each of the following chapters in this book begins with a short text section, which includes directions to guide you through the forms. That section is followed by the forms themselves.

Here is your easy-to-use guide to preparing a form:

- Start by reading the introduction to determine whether there are any special instructions you should follow. The special instructions may include making duplicate copies of the form, using registered mail, having the signing of the form witnessed or notarized or using the company letterhead.
- These forms may be used as is. Of course, new forms, based on those in the book, but with changes or modifications, also can be prepared. If the form indicates that you should use either your company or a personal letterhead, we've left enough room on the page for you to copy the form on your stationery.
- Immediately put the form back into the book—do not set it aside for later filing because it may be lost before it gets put back into the book.
- Fill in all of the blanks: the date of the agreement, the names of the parties, all contract terms. If the form has provisions that you feel are not needed, just put a line through the unnecessary material and initial it (make sure the other person initials it also).
- If last-minute changes must be made to the agreement, simply write them in and have both parties initial the changes either in the margin beside the change or immediately above or below the change.

- If the signing of the agreement must be witnessed or notarized, do *not* sign it unless you are in the presence of the witness or notary public.
- If the agreement will be completed (signed) using the mails, always send two original copies to the other party and have one returned to you. If you are uncomfortable about signing the agreement before the other person signs, simply send an unsigned copy to the other person and have him or her return it to you. Then you can make a duplicate, sign the duplicate and return the complete agreement to the other person.
- Retain the contract in your file for at least seven years. Even if the time during which a lawsuit on a contract may be brought may be less than six years in your state, you should keep the contract on file for six years for tax purposes.

Signing Your Agreements

You should ensure that you are signing any agreement in your true capacity. If the agreement is for the benefit of a corporation, you must sign in your capacity as a corporate official. If you just sign your name, you can be held liable personally on the contract. If you are signing for a partnership, you should indicate that fact. If you are signing for yourself or your own unincorporated business, then you just have to sign your name.

Example 1: Assume that you are the president of a corporation and you've entered into an agreement for the corporation. You should sign as follows:

ABC, Inc.
By:

_____
Robert Jones, President

Example 2: If you are signing an agreement for the benefit of a partnership, you should use the following format:

A&B Partnership
By:

_____
Robert Jones, Partner

Using Your Attorney

This book was not written so that you no longer will need your attorney's advice and assistance. Each form in this book was drafted by an attorney and subsequently reviewed by at least one more attorney. We are confident that these forms will serve you efficiently and safely.

The forms, however, are designed for straightforward transactions. If you are faced with a more complex arrangement or one that involves large amounts of money, you would be ill-advised to try to save money by not consulting with your lawyer.

Finally, we urge you to have your lawyer go through this book. We know that he or she will approve of the forms, and when he or she does, you'll know just how much *The Complete Guide to Business Agreements* can do for you.

2

Loans and Credit Arrangements

Introduction

This chapter contains forms designed to safeguard you as you enter into loan arrangements. As the lender, you must take measures to protect the funds you may have advanced in the form of cash or credit. This protection can come in the form of additional security, such as collateral or guaranties. Furthermore, if you are lending to a corporation, you should consider securing your loan (or credit) with the personal guaranties of the corporation's shareholders or officers. Finally, if you make a business or personal loan, a security agreement granting you an interest in property (collateral) owned by the borrower can protect your loan.

Although guaranties and collateral do protect the principal of a loan, there is one fact that you should keep in mind whenever you extend cash or credit: If you have to proceed against a guarantor or against the debtor's property, the cost of doing so will cause you to lose money. Business loans should be made only if you can be confident that the borrower will repay you without forcing you to look to guarantors or collateral.

Promissory Notes

Form 201 is designed to be used for consumer loans. It provides all of the disclosures required by the federal truth-in-lending laws. Form 202 is a promissory note that can be used when the entire loan will be repaid in one payment that will be made on a specified date. Form 203 can be used for loans that are to be repaid in either one payment or installments; it also contains a provision requiring a guaranty of payment. Form 204 is an open-ended note. It calls for payment of the amount due on demand. This form of note can be very risky for borrowers because the lender can call in the loan at any time.

Forms 205 and 206 provide for installment payments. Form 205 is a short version of an installment note. Although it can be used for an arm's-length business transaction because it does not contain a guaranty, it is more likely to be used for a loan to a friend or relative. Form 206 is a highly protective note that should be used when any significant amount of money is at issue. It contains both a guaranty and an acceleration clause. Acceleration provides that should any payment be late, then the entire amount of the note may be called. Furthermore, the note provides for attorney's fees to be paid by the borrower in the event that the lender must bring legal proceedings to collect on the note.

The guaranties supplied in Forms 207 and 208 can be used in conjunction with any promissory note. They obligate the guarantor to pay in the event the note is not paid by the borrower. Form 208 is a stronger version that is designed for true arm's-length transactions because it provides for the guarantor to pay for the costs of any legal fees incurred by the lender in enforcing the guaranty and authorizes the lender to enter a confession of judgment against the guarantor. Keep in mind that the guaranty is only as good as the guarantor. If the guarantor is not financially sound, the promise he or she makes is essentially worthless.

Uniform Commercial Code Forms

Every state has adopted the Uniform Commercial Code (UCC); this set of laws regulates secured business transactions. The UCC governs checks, notes and transfer agreements for the sale of goods. It requires that if property is taken as collateral, the underlying security agreement or a UCC-1 (available at most stationery or office supply retail shops) must be filed with the appropriate state office and/or the county clerk of the borrower's locale. Failure to file the security agreement can cause you to lose the protection of your security interest. If you do not file, you will not have "perfected" your interest, and subsequent lenders (who would not have notice of your security interest) will have a claim to the secured property that is superior to your earlier but unfiled claim.

Another important reason to file involves the possibility that your debtor may file for bankruptcy. If you file, you are a secured creditor, and the property you have taken as security does not become available to other creditors of your debtor. If, however, you do not file and the borrower subsequently files for bankruptcy, your interest will not be protected; instead, your claim will be treated as an unsecured claim, and the property you thought would be available for your claim now will be available to all creditors.

The forms in this chapter have been designed to comply with UCC specifications. Forms 209 and 210 are pledge agreements. Form 209 can be used to take a pledge of any type of property; Form 210 should be used if the pledge involves shares of stock in a corporation (make sure the borrower has endorsed the shares in blank before you take them). Both forms differ from an ordinary security agreement for you will be taking actual possession of the pledged collateral. Because you have actual possession of the property, no document filings are necessary.

Form 211 informs lenders who have security interests that you plan on establishing a purchase money security interest as a result of a credit sale. The UCC grants you the priority in the proceeds of the sale, but only if you notify other secured parties within ten days of the sale.

Forms 212 and 213 subordinate your interest to the interests of other lenders. This means that you have agreed to permit your interest to become junior to those of other creditors. Why would you make your interest inferior to the claims of others? Assume you lent money to your corporation and you've taken collateral. You may be willing to subordinate your interests to those of an outsider who is willing to lend additional money to the corporation. Form 212 subordinates only a portion of the debt owed to you; Form 213 subordinates the entire amount of the monies owed to you.

Enforcing Payments

All of the forms in this section should be placed on your letterhead, either business or personal, depending on whether you made the underlying loan in your name or in the name of your business.

Form 214 states that the borrower has made full payment on the debt. Form 215 notifies the borrower that he or she is in default on the loan because of nonpayment. If the note has endorsers, Form 216 should be used to provide them with the notice of default. Form 217 should be used to notify guarantors that the note is in default and that they must honor their guaranties. With Forms 218 through 220, you can follow the three steps required by the UCC if you must execute your security agreement. Form 218 demands possession of the collateral. Forms 219 and 220 notify the debtor that the property will be put up for sale at a public (Form 219) or private (Form 220) sale.

Form 221 is used when your borrower has paid off the loan. This form releases your security interest in the collateral. You should sign it when the debt has been paid and deliver it to your borrower, but only after the debt has been paid, i.e., after the payment check has cleared. The borrower then will file the release with the appropriate state office and clear the collateral of your security interest.

DISCLOSURE STATEMENT AND NOTE
(Federal Truth-in-Lending Act)

Date: , 19 Amount:

FOR VALUE RECEIVED, the borrower, , residing

at , shall pay to the order of

, the total amount of

dollars ($) in consecutive payments payable on the day of

the month, beginning on , 19 , until the loan is paid in

full.

Failure to make a payment when due shall be a default of the loan.

Should a default exist for more than ( ) days, the holder of

this note may cause the entire loan to be due immediately.

1. Amount of Loan:

2. Expenses:

3. Total Financed:

4. Interest Charges:

5. Total of Payments:

6. Annual Financed Percentage Rate:

SINGLE INSTALLMENT NOTE

FOR VALUE RECEIVED, the borrower,   , residing

at   , who has executed this note below, shall

pay to   (the lender or his or her assignee)

the principal amount of   dollars ($),

together with interest calculated at   percent (%), per year

on the outstanding balance. The entire amount, principal and interest,

shall be due and payable on or before   , 19   , at the follow-

ing address   .

    Failure to make a payment when due shall be a default of the loan.

Should a default exist for more than   (   ) days, the borrower agrees

to pay the holder of this note reasonable costs of collection including

attorney's fees.

Date: _____

                              Borrower: _____

NOTE AND GUARANTY

FOR VALUE RECEIVED, the Borrower, _____, residing

at _____, shall pay to the order of

_____ (Lender), at _____,

the total amount of _____ dollars ($ _____), includ-

ing principal and interest at _____ percent (_____ %) per year, in

consecutive payments, payable on the _____ day of the month beginning on

_____, until the loan is paid in full. The borrower may prepay this

loan without any early payment penalty.

Failure to make a payment when due shall be a default of the loan.

Should a default exist for more than _____ (___) days, the total amount

outstanding may be currently due, and the borrower agrees to pay the

holder of this note reasonable costs of collection including attorney's

fees.

Date: _____

Borrower: _____

GUARANTY

FOR VALUABLE CONSIDERATION RECEIVED, the guarantor, _____,

guarantees full payment of the above amount and shall remain liable until

the note is fully satisfied and paid in full.

Date: _____

Guarantor: _____

Address: _____

DEMAND NOTE

FOR VALUE RECEIVED, the borrower, _____, residing

at _____, who has executed this note below, shall

pay to _____ (the lender or his or her assignee)

the principal amount of _____ dollars ($_____),

together with interest calculated at _____ percent (____%) per year

on the outstanding balance. The entire amount, principal and interest,

shall be due and payable ON DEMAND by holder of this note.

Failure to make a payment when due shall be a default of the loan.

Should a default exist for more than _____ (____) days, the borrower agrees

to pay the holder of this note reasonable costs of collection including

attorney's fees, as authorized by state law.

Date: _____

Borrower: _____

PROMISSORY INSTALLMENT NOTE

Date:

FOR GOOD AND VALUABLE CONSIDERATION, the undersigned,

, residing at   ,

jointly and severally, and described hereafter as "Makers," hereby promise

to pay to   (hereinafter "Payee"), the sum of

dollars ($) plus interest at the rate

of   percent (%) per annum, compounded monthly, payable

in   (   ) monthly installments.

Payments: The first payment is due on   and monthly payments

thereafter on each and every first day of the month until the balance of

this note is fully paid. Each monthly payment is to be delivered to and

payable to the Payees at   , either in person

or by U.S. mail, and said monthly payments must be received by the Payees

prior to or on the due date of the monthly payments.

Default: In case of default of any monthly payments, the entire unpaid

balance, at the election of the Payees, shall become immediately due and

collectible plus attorney's fees. Default shall be defined as the Makers

being more than one (1) month in arrears on the payments due under this

note.

Prepayment Option: The Makers hereby have the right to prepay the prin-

cipal due on this note at any time without penalty.

Open Account Settlement: This note acknowledges that an outstanding account balance exists with the Payees. This note is additional security and not a separate debt.

_____

_____

WITNESS:

_____

PROMISSORY INSTALLMENT NOTE
(LONG FORM)

Date:

THE UNDERSIGNED,   , residing at

           , jointly and severally referred to as the

"Makers," for value received, hereby promises to pay to

                        (hereinafter "Payee"), the sum of

                  dollars ($) plus interest at the rate

of   percent (%) per annum, compounded monthly, payable in

        (   ) monthly installments of   dollars

($).

Payments: The first payment is due on   , and monthly payments

thereafter on each and every first day of the month until the balance of

this note is fully paid. Each monthly payment is to be delivered to and

payable to the Payee, at   , either in person

or by U.S. mail, and said monthly payment must be received by the Payee

prior to or on the due date of the monthly payments.

Default: In case of default of any monthly payment, the entire unpaid

balance, at the election of the Payee, shall become immediately due and

collectible. Default shall be defined as the Makers being more than one

(1) month in arrears on the payments due under this note.

Confession of Judgment: Makers irrevocably authorize any attorney of

any court of record to appear for Makers at any time to waive the issuance and service of process and to confess judgment against Makers and in favor of Payee or any subsequent holder hereof for such amount as is unpaid with accrued interest, together with costs and attorney's fees of thirty-three and one-third percent (33 1/3%) of the full amount due hereon (but not less than $100), and hereby ratifies and confirms all that said attorney may do by virtue hereof, and waives and releases all errors that may intervene in such proceedings. Venue shall lie in the following jurisdiction:

Collateral Security: As collateral security for the payments of this note, the Makers will execute a Stock Pledge Agreement granting Payee a security interest in the capital stock of
Inc., purchased from Payee this date, and shall deliver said shares of capital stock pursuant to such Stock Pledge Agreement.

Prepayment Option: The Makers hereby have the right to prepay the principal due on this note at any time without penalty.

_____

_____

WITNESS:

_____

GUARANTY

Date:

FOR CONSIDERATION RECEIVED, and as further incentive for

(hereinafter "Creditor") to advance credit to

residing at

(hereinafter "Borrower"), the undersigned (hereinafter "Guarantor")

jointly and severally guarantee complete and timely payment of the liabil-

ity that the Borrower owes to the Creditor. That liability is as follows:

Upon nonpayment by the Borrower of a payment properly due and owing to

the Creditor, the Creditor may move against the Guarantor without the need

to move first against the Borrower.

Furthermore, the Guarantor shall continue to be obligated on this guar-

anty, until it is revoked in writing by both the Guarantor and the Guaran-

tor is released by the Creditor.

This agreement shall be binding and shall attach to the successors and

assigns of the Guarantor.

By: _____

    Guarantor

_____

Address

NOTICE TO SECURED PARTY
OF PURCHASE MONEY SECURITY INTEREST

Date:

To:

Dear   :

Please be advised that we have or will shortly have a purchase money

security interest in the following secured collateral:

    The property listed above will be sold to:

to satisfy our claim.

    We are providing this notice to you, as a holder of a security inter-

est, of our claim of priority in the collateral.

                        Sincerely,

                    _____

SUBORDINATION AGREEMENT (PARTIAL)

FOR VALUABLE CONSIDERATION, receipt of which is acknowledged, the

creditor,   , hereby agrees to subordinate to

(Senior Creditor) our claim against

(Debtor) up to the following amount:

dollars ($).

Signed this   day of   , 19   .

Creditor: _____

Agreed to:

Debtor: _____

SUBORDINATION AGREEMENT (FULL)

FOR VALUABLE CONSIDERATION, receipt of which is acknowledged,

_____ (Creditor), the beneficiary of a security

interest granted by _____ (Debtor), dated

_____ , hereby agrees to subordinate to

_____ (Senior Creditor) the Creditor's security

interest against the Debtor up to the following amount:

_____ dollars ($ _____).

Signed this _____ day of _____, 19 _____ .

Creditor: _____

Agreed to:

Debtor: _____

RECEIPT ACKNOWLEDGING PAYMENT IN FULL

_____

RECEIPT of   dollars ($) is accepted as

complete payment in satisfaction of the outstanding claim from

, the Debtor, for the following obligation:

Signed this   day of   , 19   .

Creditor: _____

NOTICE OF PROMISSORY NOTE DEFAULT

_____

Date:

To:

PURSUANT to the terms of a certain promissory note dated

, you have failed to make the required payment. Failure

to pay constitutes a default of the note.

   PURSUANT to the note, the entire amount, including interest,

            dollars ($), is now due and payable.

   Should you not correct the default or pay the entire outstanding amount

within   (   ) days from the date of this letter, this matter

will be forwarded to our counsel for appropriate collection actions.

            Sincerely,

_____

NOTICE TO ENDORSERS OF DEFAULT ON NOTE

_____

Date:

To:

PURSUANT to the terms of a certain promissory note dated

, the borrower has failed to make the required payment.

Failure to pay constitutes a default of the note.

PURSUANT to the note, the entire amount, including interest,

dollars ($) is now due and payable.

You are the endorser of the note. Should you not correct the default or

pay the entire outstanding amount in the following   (   )

days, this matter will be forwarded for appropriate collection actions.

Sincerely,

_____

NOTICE TO GUARANTOR OF DEFAULT ON NOTE

_____

Date:

To:

PURSUANT to the terms of a certain promissory note dated

, the borrower has failed to make the required

payment. Failure to pay constitutes a default of the note.

PURSUANT to the note, the entire amount, including interest,

dollars ($) is now due and payable.

You are the guarantor of the note. Should you not pay the entire

outstanding amount in the following   (   ) days, this matter

will be forwarded for appropriate collection actions.

Sincerely,

_____

SECURED PARTY'S DEMAND FOR COLLATERAL

Date:

To:

PURSUANT to the terms of a certain security agreement and promissory note

dated   , you are in default due to your failure to:

Therefore, you must turn over the collateral to my representative

pursuant to the security agreement and the Uniform Commercial Code.

Sincerely,

PUBLIC SALE NOTICE

_____

Date:

To:

PURSUANT to the terms of a certain security agreement and promissory note

dated   , you are hereby notified that the property

held as collateral will be sold at an auction open to the public. The

date, time and place of the auction are:

Date:

Time:

Place:

In the event that the sale of the collateral at the auction does not

provide sufficient funds to satisfy the underlying debt, you will continue

to be responsible for any remaining deficiency.

Your property may be reclaimed by paying the entire amount due before

the sale.

Sincerely,

_____

PRIVATE SALE NOTICE

_____

Date:

To:

PURSUANT to the terms of a certain security agreement and promissory note

dated   , you are hereby notified that the property

held as collateral under the security agreement and promissory note will

be sold at a private sale on   , 19   .

The property to be sold at the private sale consists of:

The private buyer shall be   .

You will continue to be responsible for any deficiency if the proceeds

of the sale are insufficient to satisfy the full amount of your debt.

Your property may be reclaimed by paying the entire amount due before

the sale.

Sincerely,

_____

SECURITY INTEREST RELEASE

FOR VALUABLE CONSIDERATION RECEIVED, the secured party releases the lien created by a certain security interest, dated   ,

granted by   (debtor) to   ,

the secured party.

This release is a complete release of all liens created by the above-noted security interest.

Dated: _____

_____

Secured Party

3

Setting Up Your Credit and Collection Program

Introduction

The current business environment demands that virtually every business establish a well-managed credit and collection program. This chapter provides you with an extensive list of forms that will guide you through the processes you should follow to minimize the impact of bad-debt write-offs. The forms address the three functions of a credit and collection program: granting credit, monitoring your credit accounts and collecting outstanding accounts in a timely fashion.

Granting Credit

Forms 301 and 302 are credit applications. Federal lending laws limit what you may ask of a consumer borrower. Form 301 should be used when consumers ask for credit, for that form satisfies the federal government's requirement. Form 302 can be used for your business customers.

In the event that you are seeking credit and an incorrect, unfavorable credit report has been made, the Fair Credit Reporting Act provides you with a right to correct any errors and to demand that a copy of your request be attached to any report that the credit reporting agency issues to its clients. Form 303 asserts your rights under the Fair Credit Reporting Act.

In the event that you decide to reject a credit application, Form 304 can be used to explain your decision to the applicant. Form 305 should be used to inform a customer that he or she has exceeded his or her credit limit and advises the customer that payment must accompany any future orders or that you will ship future orders cash on delivery (COD). You may wish to consider modifying this form and using the modification if a customer is approaching his or her credit limit.

Monitoring Processes

Form 306 provides a formal structure for your company's receivables department to report the status of accounts. Your company's internal procedures should require the person who prepares the report to sign it. The form also requires the person preparing the report to recommend a future course of action with respect to the customer named in the report. The credit manager's recommendations should be reviewed and acted on.

Forms 307 through 313 should be on business letterhead stationery. Form 307 is the first of a series of letters you can use to collect overdue accounts. Form 308 is a friendly letter designed to make your customer come forward. At this point, you can assume that you may be able to work out an arrangement that will not injure the business relationship that you have with your customer.

Forms 309 and 310 are follow-up notices that should be used if your company has not received a response to Forms 307 or 308. Form 310 (the Final Overdue Notice) should be sent by certified mail with a return receipt requested.

If the customer's response to any of these form letters is to suggest installment payments of the outstanding balance on his or her account, form 311 should be used to memorialize any agreement that you may have worked out with the customer. Remember, this form is a contract between you and your debtor. You must, therefore, send a signed original and a signed copy of the letter agreement to the customer and require him or her to return a signed copy to you. In other words, both copies should be signed as originals.

If all other efforts have failed, then you should forward your collection problem (include copies of unpaid invoices and your collection letters) to your attorney or collection agency. Form 312 can be used for this purpose. Form 313 should be used to ensure that your lawyer or collection agency keeps your account at the top of its work list. Remember, attorneys and collection agencies work for you; do not be shy about asking for updates. Form 314 can be an important weapon in the event that you will have to sue to collect the debt. In this form, the customer admits that he or she owes you money. If used early in the collection process, the customer may be willing to sign it to stay in your good graces. If it eventually becomes necessary to sue, the customer's admission of the debt in Form 314 can prevent him or her from challenging the legitimacy of your claim.

Payment Forms

Form 315 should be used to acknowledge cash payment from a customer. Form 316 replaces a check from a customer. The customer is authorizing his or her bank to pay you out of the named account. Ordinarily, this form is used when you meet with a customer and he or she agrees to pay but does not happen to be carrying a check. If the customer promises to mail the check when he or she gets back to the office, you can use the Bank Draft Order set out in Form 316 to obtain payment on the spot. If the customer objects, you may want to take the customer's promise to mail a check with a grain of salt.

Form 317 notifies your customer that a check he or she gave you was not honored by the bank. Before using Form 317, you should call your local law enforcement authorities, either the police department or the county prosecutor's office. In many states, writing a bad check is a crime. Although Form 317 may be the only notice that is required for you to be entitled to file a criminal complaint, your jurisdiction may have additional requirements.

CONSUMER CREDIT APPLICATION

Name: Social Security #:

Street:

City: State: Zip Code:

Telephone:

Employer: Supervisor:

Employer's Address: Telephone:

Annual Salary: Years Employed:

Position:

Additional Income:

Personal:

Date of Birth: Dependents:

Home: Owned   Rented   Live with parents

Mortgage holder or Landlord: Monthly Payment:

Credit Sources:

Did you ever declare bankruptcy or have a judgment filed against you?

If yes, list the court and date:

Bank:

    Checking Account:

    Savings Account:

    Bank Address:

Credit Cards (list account number, balance and monthly payment):

Visa:

Mastercard:

American Express:

Diners Club:

Discover:

SIGNATURE (ALL APPLICANTS)

The information contained in this application is true and complete, and is supplied to obtain credit from you. I authorize you to verify any and every aspect of the information in the application and any additional information that you may require in connection with this application or in connection with any review, update, extension, renewal or collection of any credit you extend as a result of this application. I also authorize you to report your credit experience with me to others such as banks, retail establishments and credit-reporting agencies.

KEEPING APPLICATION: The undersigned agrees that this application may be retained whether or not you approve it.

ACKNOWLEDGMENT: The undersigned acknowledges receipt of a Notice Regarding Credit Reports.

Applicant 1 Signature: _____ Date: _____

Applicant 2 Signature: _____ Date: _____

CREDIT APPLICATION FOR A BUSINESS

Name of Business:

Type of Business: General Partnership   Corporation

                          Limited Partnership   Sole Proprietorship

Address:

Federal ID# or Social Security #:

Partners/Owner/President:

Address:

Telephone: (Home)   (Business)

Date Business Started:

Dun and Bradstreet Rating:

Amount of Credit Requested:

Bank: Account #:

Credit References:

Trade References:

   Are you a defendant in a lawsuit? Yes No (Circle one.) If so, list and

describe the lawsuits:

The undersigned consents to the release of credit history. We recognize that if credit is extended, it may be canceled without notice.

_____

NOTICE CORRECTING CREDIT INFORMATION

_____

Date:

To:

Gentlemen/Mesdames:

It has come to my attention that the following negative information is

listed on my credit history:

That data is incorrect in the following aspects:

Pursuant to the Fair Credit Reporting Act, I ask that this letter be

attached to my credit history and that it be included with any response

that your company makes to any and all credit requests made on my account.

Kindly receipt and return the enclosed copy of this letter.

Your prompt cooperation is greatly appreciated.

Sincerely,

_____

Social Security #: _____

EXPLANATION OF CREDIT REJECTION

_____

Date:

To:

On _____, 19____, you requested an explanation of why your application for credit was refused. Our reasons for declining to extend credit to you are based on the following information that we received:

We appreciate your past patronage and welcome your future patronage; if you believe the above information is incorrect in any fashion, please do not hesitate to write to us at your convenience.

Sincerely,

_____

CREDIT LIMIT NOTIFICATION

_____

Date:

To:

Reviewing your account, we have noted that you have a current outstanding

account balance of   dollars ($). Your ac-

count limit has been set at   dollars ($).

   You are currently in excess of your account limitation. Your business

is important to us; however, until you reduce your outstanding account

balance, future orders will be shipped either prepaid or cash on delivery

(COD).

   If you believe your situation justifies an increase in your account

limit, we would be pleased to discuss it with you.

                    Sincerely,

                    _____

ACCOUNTS RECEIVABLE REPORT

Client:

Client Number:

Address:

Receivables analysis:

Less than 30 days:

30 to 60 days:

61 to 90 days:

Over 90 days:

Total outstanding:

Payment agreement with client: Yes No (Circle one.) If a payment agreement exists, set out the terms:

If no payment agreement exists, circle one of the recommended actions listed below:

Continue to ship

Require payment plan

Ship cash on delivery (COD)

Turn over for collection action

Accounts Receivable Department

OVERDUE NOTICE

_____

Date:

To:

Have you forgotten us? Our bill, dated   , 19   , was due on

       , 19   . If you have mailed your payment, please disregard

this notice and accept our sincere thanks.

   If not, please mail your check in the amount of

dollars ($) today.

   Thank you.

                    Sincerely,

                    _____

PAYMENT INFORMATION REQUEST

_____

Date:

To:

Dear   :

Our accounts receivable department recently advised me that it has been un-

successful in making arrangements with you on your past due account. Your

current past due amount is   dollars ($).

   You are a valued customer and we would like to retain our relationship

with you. However, we must have some agreement with respect to your

account. Kindly give me a call so that we may arrange mutually agreeable

terms.

                         Sincerely,

                         _____

SECOND OVERDUE NOTICE

_____

Date:

To:

Dear   :

We wrote to you about your past due bill on   , 19   . We have

not as of yet received payment.

    If you have mailed your payment, please disregard this notice and

accept our sincere thanks. If not, please mail your check in the amount of

                        dollars ($) today.

    If we do not receive payment within ten (10) working days of the date

of this letter, we shall be obliged to take appropriate action to enforce

our rights.

    Thank you.

                    Sincerely,

                    _____

FINAL OVERDUE NOTICE

Date:

To:

Dear   :

We wrote to you on   , 19   , and again on   ,

19   ,   about your past due bill in the amount of

dollars ($).

   We have not as of yet received payment. If we do not receive payment

within seven (7) business days, we will be forced to turn your account

over to a collection agency. Such action may impact your credit history in

an unfavorable fashion.

   If you have mailed your payment, please disregard this notice and

accept our sincere thanks.

                              Sincerely,

                              _____

INSTALLMENT ACCOUNT SETTLEMENT

_____

Date:

To:

Dear   :

We are pleased to settle your outstanding receivable by agreeing to an installment plan whereby you will pay off the outstanding balance in installments of   dollars ($) per   .
Under this agreement, your first payment will be due on   ,
19   .

   We look forward to your future business. If this meets with your understanding, kindly sign the enclosed copy of this letter agreement under the
words "Agreed to and accepted" and return that signed copy to us.

   Thank you.

                         Sincerely,

                         _____

Agreed to and accepted:

_____

COLLECTION DISPATCH

Date:

To:

Dear   :

Enclosed are the following outstanding accounts. Kindly begin the appropriate collection proceedings.

Customer   Invoice Number   Outstanding Balance

Please advise of any and all actions that you take with respect to the above accounts receivable.

Sincerely,

COLLECTION EFFORTS UPDATE

_____

Date:

To:

Kindly report on your efforts regarding the following accounts that we

transmitted to your office in a letter dated   , 19   :

Customer   Invoice Number   Outstanding Balance

Sincerely,

_____

ACKNOWLEDGMENT OF ACCOUNT BALANCE

Date:

The undersigned agrees that he or she owes to

the amount of   dollars ($). Furthermore,

I agree that there are no credits or setoffs that have not been reflected

in my account.

_____

Customer

RECEIPT

Receipt of _____ dollars ($ _____) is hereby acknowledged. Said amount was paid in (circle one): cash   check number:

_____ .

Date: _____

_____

BANK DRAFT ORDER

Date:

To:

Pay to the order of   (Payee) the sum of

dollars ($).

_____

Drawer of Draft

_____

Bank Account Number

OVERDRAFT CHECK NOTICE

_____

Date:

To:

Dear   :

Your check number   , in the amount of

dollars ($) has been returned by your bank as uncollectible

funds. You must make this check good within   (   ) days. Should we

not receive such funds promptly, we shall pursue all appropriate legal

actions.

                    _____

                                                        .

Leasing Commercial Space

Introduction

This chapter will provide the forms necessary for simple landlord-tenant situations. In the relatively uncomplicated lease transaction, the parties themselves can satisfy their needs using the forms in this chapter. More complicated lease arrangements, however, should be drafted by a professional because the variables are so great that even the smallest error can prove far more costly than the fee that your attorney will charge for his or her efforts.

Leases

Form 401 sets out a simple lease that is useful in most business situations. Form 402 provides a recordable document that will protect the tenant in the event that your building is purchased. Read your lease carefully and make certain that it does not prohibit you from filing this form.

Form 403 will document any lease revisions agreed to by both the landlord and the tenant. In the event that the landlord and the tenant agree to extend the lease beyond its expiration date, Form 404 can be used to document that agreement.

Form 405 permits one tenant to transfer (assign) his or her rights under a lease to another tenant. Before entering into such an agreement (whether you are assigning or taking an assignment), examine the lease to ensure that it can be assigned. You will note that the form also calls for the landlord to sign the assignment. By obtaining the landlord's signature on the assignment, the parties avoid any possibility that the landlord will object to the new tenant.

If the landlord and the tenant agree to terminate a lease, Form 406 documents that agreement and protects both parties from any subsequent disagreement on the question of whether there was such an agreement.

Fixtures and Lease Terminations

Form 407 protects the tenant's right to fixtures that he or she may have installed on the leased property. Local property law may grant title to the landlord for fixtures installed. This form establishes the tenant's rights to such property. If you are a tenant and you intend to improve the property that you are renting, you should use this form. One of the most frequently litigated issues involving landlords and tenants involves the question of who owns the improvements made by the tenants.

Form 408, which should be on the tenant's business stationery, provides the landlord with notice that the tenant is ending an at-will tenancy. A prudent tenant will either ask the landlord to return a signed copy of the form or send the notice by certified mail with a return receipt requested.

Form 409 can be used by the landlord to demand that the tenant vacate the premises based on the tenant's failure to pay rent. Note that the form demands that the tenant leave the rented property in broom-clean condition. Prudent landlords send this form by certified mail and request a return receipt in order to avoid any claim by the tenant that the landlord acted without notice.

Form 410 is a mirror image of Form 408. In Form 410, the landlord provides notice to the tenant that an at-will tenancy will terminate. Although not required by most state laws, this notice should be sent by certified mail with a return receipt requested.

LEASE AGREEMENT

LEASE AGREEMENT made this   day of   , 19   , between

                    , with an address at

                    (hereinafter referred to as "Landlord") and

                    , with an address at

                    (hereinafter referred to as "Tenant").

It is therefore agreed:

1.   Premises: The Landlord shall lease to the Tenant the premises

     located at:

2.   Lease Term: The term of this lease shall be for a period of

     (   ) year(s), commencing   , 19   , and terminating

              , 19   . The lease term can be extended only by

     mutual agreement of the parties hereto.

3.   Rental Amount: The Tenant shall pay to the Landlord an annual sum

     of   dollars ($) to lease the

     property. Rental payments shall be paid in monthly payments, each

     of which shall be in the amount of

     dollars ($), and each of which shall be paid on the

          day of the month.

4.   Option To Renew: The Tenant shall have an option to renew this

     lease on the premises for a   (   )-year period upon the

     following terms and conditions:

     The Tenant's option to renew must be exercised in writing and must be received by the Landlord no less than ( ) days before the expiration of this lease or any extensions thereof.

5. Arbitration: Any controversy or claim arising out of or relating to this lease agreement or the breach thereof shall be settled by arbitration in accordance with the rules then obtaining of the American Arbitration Association, and judgment upon the award rendered may be entered and enforced in any court having jurisdiction thereof.

6. No Violation or Breach: The Landlord and the Tenant warrant and represent each to the other that the performance of this agreement does not violate any laws, statutes, local ordinances, state or federal regulations, regarding controlled substances, or otherwise, or any court order or administrative order or ruling, nor is such performance in violation of any loan document's conditions or restrictions in effect for financing, whether secured or unsecured.

7. Benefit: This agreement shall be binding upon and inure to the benefit of the parties hereto and their legal representatives, successors and assigns.

8. Notices: Any notice required or desired to be given under this agreement shall be deemed given if in writing sent by certified mail to the addresses of the parties to this lease agreement as follows:

Landlord:

Tenant:

9. Captions: Captions are used in this agreement for convenience only and are not intended to be used in the construction or in the interpretation of this agreement.

10. Invalid Provision: In the event any provision of this agreement is held to be void, invalid or unenforceable in any respect, then the same shall not affect the remaining provisions hereof, which shall continue in full force and effect.

11. Entire Agreement: This agreement contains the entire understanding of the parties. It may not be changed orally. This agreement may be amended or modified only in writing that has been executed by both parties hereto.

12. Interpretation: This lease agreement shall be interpreted under the laws of the state of   .

Landlord

By:

_____

_____

Tenant

LEASE NOTICE

ANNOUNCEMENT of the duration of the following lease is hereby made:

1. Landlord:

2. Tenant:

3. Property leased:

4. Duration of lease:

5. Optional terms:

    (a) Right to acquire:

    (b) Right of first refusal on sale:

    (c) Right to lease extension:

                        Landlord

                        By:

                        _____

                        _____

                        Tenant

_____

(Notary Public)

LEASE AMENDMENT

FOR CONSIDERATION MUTUALLY EXCHANGED between the parties,

(hereinafter "Landlord") and

(hereinafter "Tenant"), this lease amend-

ment is made this   day of   , 19   .

WHEREAS, the Landlord and the Tenant have previously entered into a

lease agreement dated   ; and

WHEREAS, both parties desire to amend the lease;

NOW, therefore intending to be legally bound, both parties agree as

follows:

In all other respects, said lease shall continue in full force and

effect.

IN WITNESS WHEREOF, the parties have executed this lease amendment the

day and year first above written.

Landlord

By:

_____

_____

Tenant

LEASE EXTENSION

FOR CONSIDERATION MUTUALLY EXCHANGED between the parties,

(hereinafter "Landlord") and

(hereinafter "Tenant"), this extension

agreement is made this   day of   , 19   .

WHEREAS, the Landlord and the Tenant previously entered into a lease

dated   , 19   ; and

WHEREAS, said agreement will conclude on   , 19   ; and

WHEREAS, both parties desire to extend the lease;

NOW, therefore intending to be legally bound, both parties agree as

follows:

1. The agreement shall be lengthened for an additional term of

    .

2. During the duration of this extension, the monthly rent shall be

    in the amount of   dollars ($).

3. In all other respects, said lease shall continue in full force and

    effect.

IN WITNESS WHEREOF, the parties have executed this agreement the day and year first above written.

Landlord

By:

_____

_____

Tenant

LEASE ASSIGNMENT AGREEMENT

AGREEMENT entered into this _____ day of _____, 19 ___ , by and be-

tween _____ (hereinafter "Assignor") and

_____, (hereinafter "Assignee") and

_____ (hereinafter "Landlord").

WHEREAS, the Assignor is the tenant of leased premises located at

_____; and

WHEREAS, the Assignor desires to assign said lease rights to

_____; and

WHEREAS, the Assignee desires to acquire said lease.

NOW, THEREFORE, for good and valuable consideration, the parties hereto

agree as follows:

1. Sale of Lease. The Assignor shall assign it rights in the above-

    mentioned lease to the Assignee. The lease representing said lease-

    hold interest is attached hereto and made a part hereof as Exhibit

    "A."

2. Purchase Price. The purchase price for the sale of the lease

    rights as described in paragraph 1 above shall be

    _____ dollars ($ _____). The Assignee shall

    tender to the Landlord a check in the amount of

    _____ dollars ($ _____).

3. Date the Assignor Shall Vacate the Leased Premises. The Assignor

    shall vacate the leased premises no later than _____ ,

19 ___ . The Assignor may vacate the leased premises prior to

___ , 19 ___ , provided that the Assignor notifies the Land-

lord and the Assignee of such occurrence at least ___ (___)

weeks prior to the date of vacate. The leased premises shall be

left in broom-clean condition, and the Assignor shall, prior to

the date of vacate, remove from the leased premises all items of

personalty belonging to the Assignor.

4. Proration of Rent. The Assignee hereby agrees to reimburse the

Assignor for all rents paid by the Assignor to the Landlord that

represent rental payments for the period of time after the date of

vacate by the Assignor.

5. Waiver of Breach. The waiver by any party to this agreement of a

breach of any provision of this agreement by any party shall not

operate or be construed as a waiver of any subsequent breach by

any party. No waiver shall be valid unless in writing and signed

by the parties to this agreement.

6. Captions. Captions are used in this agreement for convenience only

and are not intended to be used in the construction or in the in-

terpretation of this agreement.

7. Interpretation. This agreement shall be interpreted in accordance

with the laws of the state of ___ .

8. Enforceability. In the event that any provision of this agreement

is held to be void, invalid or unenforceable in any respect, then the same shall not affect the remaining provisions or subprovisions hereof, which shall continue in full force and effect.

9. <u>Binding Effect.</u> This agreement shall bind the parties hereto, their legal representatives, successors and assigns. The Assignee assumes and undertakes all of the terms and conditions of the lease as its own obligations.

10. <u>Entire Agreement.</u> This agreement contains the entire understanding of the parties. It may not be changed orally. This agreement may be amended or modified only with such writing being executed by the parties hereto.

IN WITNESS WHEREOF, the parties have caused this agreement to be executed on the date first above written.

Landlord

By:

_____

Assignor

By:

_____

Assignee

By:

_____

AGREED LEASE TERMINATION

FOR CONSIDERATION MUTUALLY EXCHANGED between the parties,

and   , this

agreement is made this   day of   , 19   .

    WHEREAS,   and

previously entered into a lease dated   , 19   ; and

    WHEREAS, both parties desire to terminate the lease;

    NOW THEREFORE, intending to be legally bound, both parties agree as

follows:

    1.   Said lease shall cease as of   , 19   .

    2.   Both parties agree to release each other of all liability under

         the lease, except for such obligations that arose prior to the can-

         cellation date set out in paragraph 1 above.

    3.   In all other respects, said agreement shall continue in full force

         and effect.

    IN WITNESS WHEREOF, the parties have executed this agreement the day

and year first above written.

WITNESS:

_____

                        _____

                        Landlord

                        _____

                        Tenant

LANDLORD'S WAIVER OF CLAIM TO FIXTURES

FOR VALUABLE CONSIDERATION, receipt of which is acknowledged,

_____ (hereinafter "Landlord") hereby surrenders

any claim to personal property that has been affixed to the real property

located at _____ and leased by

_____ (hereinafter "Tenant") under a lease dated

_____, 19____, a copy of which is attached hereto. Furthermore, the

Landlord also surrenders any claim to any personal property installed on

the property by the Tenant, even if such property may be deemed to be a

fixture upon the property.

The Landlord acknowledges and admits that said fixtures retain their

status of personal property and may be removed by the Tenant.

Dated: _____

_____
Landlord

_____
Tenant

TENANT'S NOTICE ENDING AT-WILL TENANCY

_____

Date:

To:

Dear   :

I am your tenant at will in your property located at:

                              .

   By means of this letter, you are hereby informed that the tenancy will

end on   , 19   , and that the premises will be vacated on or

before that date.

   Please acknowledge your receipt of this notice by returning the

enclosed copy of this letter to the undersigned at the address shown above.

                              Sincerely,

                    _____

                              Tenant

Receipt Acknowledged:

_____

Landlord

NOTICE TO VACATE FOR FAILURE TO PAY RENT

_____

Date:

To:

Dear   :

You are the tenant of premises located at

and occupy the premises under a lease dated   , 19   .

    The above-mentioned lease calls on you to make monthly rental payments

of   dollars ($). You are now in arrears

in the amount of   dollars ($), having

failed and refused to pay your rent since   , 19   , as you are

obligated to do under the terms of the above-mentioned lease.

    Accordingly, you are required to pay the above sum within three (3)

days after you receive this notice or surrender possession of the premises

in a broom-clean condition to the Landlord. Your failure to comply will

result in the Landlord commencing eviction proceedings under the statute

to recover possession of the premises.

                        Sincerely,

                        _____

                        Landlord

                        By:

                        _____

LANDLORD'S NOTICE ENDING AT-WILL TENANCY

_____

Date:

To:

Dear   :

You are the tenant occupying the property located at:

                    , under the terms of a lease dated   ,

19   .

Your tenancy under that lease is a tenancy at will. You are hereby

advised that your tenancy shall end on   , 19   , and you are

hereby directed to vacate the leased premises no later than that date.

We also remind you that under the terms of the lease, you are required

to leave the premises in broom-clean condition.

Sincerely,

_____

Landlord

5

The Employment Relationship

Introduction

This chapter provides forms designed to safeguard your business in its employment practices, starting with an employee's hiring until the time he or she leaves your employ. Essentially, the forms address ordinary work relationships. As a practical matter, they cannot address specific federal laws that can affect the employment relationship. For example, despite the existence of a valid contract, your company still must satisfy many state and federal laws bearing on the employment relationship. For instance, an employee who is covered by minimum wage laws cannot waive his or her right to that minimum wage, even if an otherwise valid contract provides for a lower pay scale.

Similarly, an employment contract cannot waive an employee's right to be free of discriminatory treatment on the job. Keep in mind that federal and state antidiscrimination laws cover employees who are treated unfairly because of age, race, national origin, physical handicap, religion or sex. Furthermore, the reach of these laws—at both the state and federal level—is very long. The case books are filled with litigation involving relatively small firms that have been forced to rehire former employees at higher levels and even provide back pay for a year or more that the employees were not on the payroll.

Initial Employment

Form 501 should be written on your company's stationery. It is directed to a job applicant's former employer and asks for references. Do not be surprised if the response is limited to an acknowledgment that the individual was employed during a certain time period. Many employers are unwilling to respond more fully because they fear that their former employees might sue them if references contain anything that might be construed as unfavorable, even if the references are completely truthful. If your written requests do not yield more than a list of previous employment dates, you may wish to consider telephoning prior employers. One simple way to get around their reluctance to answer specific questions is to ask whether the former employees are qualified to be rehired by their companies. If the answer is no, you may want to reconsider the applicant's potential for your company.

Form 502 is an in-house evaluation format that you should adopt to ensure that all job applicants go through the same process and that every aspect of your hiring process (including credential checking) is followed.

If your company requires job applicants to undergo a medical examination, you must protect yourself by keeping a written consent from each applicant in your permanent files. Form 503 is designed for just this purpose.

Form 504 provides a simple, letter-format employment contract for employment at will. An at-will employee is one who can quit at any time and who can be fired at any time. Many states still recognize that employment without a contract is an "at-will" relationship. There is a growing trend in some courts, however, to hold that employees who do not have a written agreement and who have long-term tenure cannot be fired at the employer's will. Form 504 confirms the at-will nature of the relationship and strengthens the employer's position when a long-term, at-will employee is fired.

Caveat: Even if an employment contract states an employee is hired at will, many courts nevertheless will incorporate the provisions of your employee handbook (or other rules published by the employer) into the at-will contract. If your employee handbook provides that an employee cannot be fired unless a specified procedure is followed, then the courts may well conclude that you cannot fire the employee at your will, but that you must follow the procedures set out in the handbook.

Form 505 is a formal employment contract for a salesperson. It contains a promise that obligates the employee not to compete with the employer after he or she leaves the company's employ. This is an employer-oriented form and many of its provisions provide additional levels of protection for the employer. Read it carefully and implement those most useful to you.

Form 506 protects the employer in the event the Internal Revenue Service disallows a payment that reimburses an employee for business expenses. It is used most often as part of an employment agreement (either standing alone or as part of the employment contract) with officers/owners and protects the employer from adverse tax treatment. Form 507 is an expense account report form. It provides a structure with which an employee can be reimbursed and will help you treat those expenses correctly for tax purposes.

Form 508 protects the employer when an agency, such as a mortgage company, bank or credit-card company, requests information about an employee. You should have the employee sign this form before you release information to protect you in the event that a disgruntled employee should seek to sue for invasion of privacy.

Noncompetition Agreements

Forms 509, 510 and 511 prohibit employees from taking clients when they leave your employ. Form 509 is a lengthy, employer-oriented, general non-competition agreement. Form 510 is a short-form version of Form 509. Form 511 restricts an employee from competing with the employer in an identified geographic region.

Tips for Protection

Form 509 suggests that you have the agreement notarized. Although notarization is not required by law, it does drive home to the employee how seriously you take the noncompetition agreement and will do away with any potential claim by the employee that he or she does not recall signing such an agreement. For the same reasons, we urge you to have Forms 510 and 511 notarized.

If they are to be upheld by the courts, noncompetition agreements must be "reasonable" as to both duration and area covered. They should not be so overly burdensome as to appear punitive. Essentially, the agreement should do no more than protect your current and reasonable future needs. For example, if your company does business throughout a 50-mile radius and you have begun plans to expand so that you can serve a 100-mile area, the noncompetition agreement should seek to protect you within a 100-, not a 50-mile radius.

With respect to the duration of a noncompetition agreement, it is clear from existing precedent that most courts will enforce agreements that restrict employees for up to one year after they leave their jobs. If the restriction lasts for a longer term, most courts will require the employers to demonstrate that the time periods are reasonable.

Terminating Employees

Forms 512, 513 and 514 have taken on increased importance in today's legal environment. Properly documenting an employee's personnel file is an absolute necessity if you want to fire an individual today. Both the Equal Employment Opportunity Act and the Age Discrimination in Employment Act grant the disgruntled employee recourse for improper termination.

The three forms provided in this section provide a format that you should follow both in form and in spirit. First, meet with the employee whose work is not up to par and explain what the problem is and how you expect the employee to correct it. Then, memorialize that meeting by using Form 512 and ensure that the employee returns a signed copy of the memo to you.

If that meeting and notice do not do the job, hold a second meeting with the employee and go through the problem and the solutions you are looking for once again. Use Form 513 to memorialize this meeting (remember to get a signed copy of the notice).

If the second meeting does not produce the desired results, then you have two options. If the employee is making an effort to comply with your wishes and you are not yet prepared to fire that person, you may wish to hold a third meeting and used a variation of Form 513 to give the employee a last chance. If you've concluded that the employee will not work out the problem, then you should use Form 514 to notify the employee that he or she is being fired.

EMPLOYMENT REFERENCE REQUEST

_____

Date:

Dear:

has applied to us seeking a position as

. Your firm has been listed by the applicant

as a prior employer.

By means of this letter, we are requesting a reference on the applicant including but not limited to the dates the applicant was employed by you, the date the individual left your employment, a rating of his or her performance and the reason the applicant left your employ.

A consent form executed by the applicant is enclosed.

Your prompt consideration is greatly appreciated.

Sincerely,

_____

APPLICANT CHECKLIST

1. Name:

2. Address:

3. Job Station:

4. References:

   <u>Previous Employers:</u>   <u>Date Requested:</u>   <u>Date Received:</u>

5. Interview Process:

   <u>Interviewer:</u>   <u>Recommendation:</u>

6. Credentials:

   <u>Education:</u>   <u>Licenses:</u>   <u>Date Validated:</u>

7. Starting Salary:

8. Benefits Package:

9. Commencement Date:

MEDICAL CONSENT

I, the undersigned individual, asserting that I am over the age of majority, in consideration for employment with _____ , do, for the limited purpose of consideration of employment, authorize the following medical examination:

I recognize that the medical examination is for the benefit of my prospective employer and will be included as a part of its determination whether to extend employment to me.

I release _____ and the medical professional who will conduct such tests from all liability for diagnosis and treatment. I authorize this consent without limitation or uncertainty.

Date: _____

_____

LETTER OF EMPLOYMENT

_____

Date:

Dear   :

It is with pleasure that we inform you of your appointment as

                              with our firm. Your immediate supervisor will

be   . The starting date of your employment is

        , 19   .

    Your annual compensation will be   dollars

($), which will be paid on a   basis.

    You will be entitled, on a yearly basis, to   (   ) days of vaca-

tion time and   (   ) days of paid sick leave.

    Furthermore, you will be a participant in the employee benefit plans to

which you are eligible. They will be explained in greater detail when you

are eligible to participate.

    THIS CONTRACT IS FOR EMPLOYMENT AT WILL. IT MAY BE TERMINATED EITHER BY

YOU OR BY US FOR ANY REASON AT ANY TIME.

    Kindly acknowledge your acceptance of this offer by signing your name

after the words "Agreed to and accepted" and return the enclosed copy of

this letter to us at the address shown above.

                              Sincerely,

                    _____

Agreed to and accepted: _____

SALES EMPLOYMENT AGREEMENT

EMPLOYMENT AGREEMENT, effective this   day of   , 19   , by

and between   (hereinafter referred to as the

"Company"), a corporation organized and existing under the laws of the

state of   , with its principal place of business located at

                              , and   ,

(hereinafter referred to as the "Employee"), an individual, with his or

her principal residence located at   .

WITNESSETH:

WHEREAS, the Company is in the business of

                              ; and

WHEREAS, the operation by the Company of its business requires disclo-

sure of confidential information to its employees; and

WHEREAS, such confidential information provided to the Employee by the

Company if improperly used by the Employee for his or her own purpose

rather than on behalf of the Company can result in irreparable harm to the

Company, which harm, because of the nature of the industry, is not suscep-

tible to precise proof; and

WHEREAS, the training of the Employee by the Company, the skills ob-

tained by the Employee and the disclosure to the Employee of such afore-

said confidential information makes such Employee valuable to competitors

of the Company; and

WHEREAS, the Employee is desirous of entering into the employment of the Company and is aware of the foregoing consideration and understands the reasons for the terms and conditions of his or her employment as set forth below.

NOW, THEREFORE, in consideration of the premises and mutual covenants and promises set forth herein, and intending to be legally bound hereby, the parties agree as follows:

ARTICLE I: PURPOSES. The Company hereby employs the Employee and the Employee accepts employment from the Company as a salesperson and/or such other duties as the Company may, from time to time, determine.

The Company hereby engages the Employee for the primary purpose of soliciting   sales in the territory or territories to be determined by the Company at the Company's sole discretion.

ARTICLE II: DUTIES. The Employee accepts such employment as a salesperson and agrees to devote his or her full-time and best efforts to soliciting sales in the territory or territories to be determined by the Company.

The Employee shall solicit   sales for the exclusive benefit of the Company and perform such other duties as may be assigned to him or her by the Company. The Employee agrees that during the term of this agreement, he or she will have no other employment except as may be specifically authorized in writing by the Company. The Employee shall not serve as an adviser, agent, consultant, independent contractor or in any other capacity with respect to any trade or business, proprietorship, partnership, corporation or other entity, person or firm that directly

sells or services   or any type of product or service

that competes, conflicts or interferes with the performance of his or her

duties, unless he or she has first received written consent of the Com-

pany, which consent shall be revocable at the will of the Company.

The Employee shall present the Company's line of

to prospective clients and will offer such   at prices

furnished by the Company, on the terms and conditions established by the

Company and in the territories established by the Company.

The Employee shall not at any time enter into any contract with any per-

son, firm or corporation that shall purport to bind the Company in any man-

ner whatsoever without written authority from the Company and any such

contract entered into by such Employee shall not be binding upon the Com-

pany. The Company specifically reserves the right to reject any contract

or to cancel any contract or part thereof even after acceptance, for

credit reasons or for any other reason whatsoever that the Company may

deem appropriate.

ARTICLE III: TERMS. The Company hereby employs the Employee and the

Employee hereby accepts employment for a term of   (   ) year(s) from

the date hereof unless terminated by either party by written notice sent

by certified mail at least   (   ) days in advance of such termination.

Such notice of termination shall not prejudice either party as to any

remedies under the provisions of this agreement. If the agreement is not terminated by either party during the initial term hereof, the Employee's employment shall continue thereafter under the terms and conditions hereof for a period of one year, and so on from year to year, until either party terminates this agreement.

ARTICLE IV: COMPENSATION. As compensation for all of the services to be rendered by the Employee pursuant to the terms and conditions set forth herein and such other duties as the Company may from time to time determine, the Employee shall receive a commission in an amount to be determined pursuant to the Schedule(s) of Commissions to be published by the Company, from time to time.

In the event that a commission is paid to the Employee pursuant to the terms of this ARTICLE IV, and the Company, for whatever reason whatsoever, is thereafter obligated to return the payments upon which the commission is determined, the Employee shall, upon thirty (30) days written notice, repay to the Company such compensation as he or she has received based on the amounts so returned or returnable. Compensation payable pursuant to this ARTICLE IV shall be paid not less frequently than monthly and may be offset by any amounts owed to the Company.

In the event the Company shall determine, in its sole discretion, that compensation based on the Schedule of Commissions shall change, the Company shall provide written notice to the Employee at least thirty (30) days prior to the said change. The Company agrees that it shall not change the commission schedule unless the said changes are made for all sales employees of the Company.

Any amounts paid and any benefits provided to the Employee pursuant to this agreement that are deemed to be compensation under the Internal Revenue Code shall be subject to the applicable income tax withholding for federal, state and local income taxes. In addition, the Company shall deduct from the compensation paid to the Employee such other deductions as authorized by the Employee or by a court of competent jurisdiction.

ARTICLE V: OTHER BENEFITS AND EXPENSES. The Employee shall be entitled during the term of this agreement to participate in all health-insurance and benefit plans, group insurance or other plan or plans providing benefits generally applicable to the employees of the Company who are currently in existence or those who hereafter may be adopted by the Company.

Once the Employee shall be deemed a "successful salesperson," said determination to be at the sole discretion of the Company as applied to all salespeople, the Employee may draw for expenses up to

dollars ($) per month, the said draw amount being subject to change as long as the said change applies to all "successful salespeople" at the sole discretion of the Company. The Employee shall submit evidence of the said expenses on no less than a monthly basis with the difference between the monthly draw and the actual verified expenses being returned to the Company within thirty (30) days of notice.

ARTICLE VI: PRICES AND SERVICE. The Employee shall sell the Company's

at the price and under the terms and conditions established by the Company. Said prices, terms and conditions may, from time to time, be changed and/or modified by the Company at its sole discretion. The Employee shall not at any time enter into any contract with any person, firm or corporation that shall purport to bind the Company in any manner whatsoever without written authority from the Company and any such contract entered into by such Employee shall not be binding upon the Company. The Company specifically reserves the right to reject any application or contract or to cancel any application or contract or part thereof even after acceptance, for credit reasons or for any other reason whatsoever that the Company deems appropriate.

ARTICLE VII: TERMINATION. In the event of the death of the Employee, the Company shall pay to the representative of the Employee's estate all funds due to the Employee to the date of death. In the event that the Employee becomes disabled because of physical or mental disability as to be unable to perform the services required by this agreement and such disability continues for   (   ) days, the Company may, at or after the expiration of such   (   )-day period and provided that the Employee's incapacity is then continuing, terminate the Employee's employment under this agreement. It is expressly understood that the inability of the Employee to render services to the Company by reason of illness, disability or incapacity or any cause beyond his or her control shall not constitute a failure by the Employee to perform his or her obligations hereunder and shall not be considered a breach or default under this agreement.

In the event that the Employee violates any of the provisions of this agreement or performs any act or does anything by which the Company shall incur liability, then, at the option of the Company, this contract shall at once cease and the Company shall be under no obligation to the Employee, except to pay the Employee for such services as may have been performed up to the date of termination of this agreement as herein provided.

In the event that the Employee violates any of the provisions of this agreement or fails to perform the services required of the Employee by this agreement, then at the option of the Company, this agreement shall at once cease and become null and void and the Company shall be under no obligation to said Employee except to pay the Employee such compensation as he or she may be entitled to receive up to the time of such termination.

In the event that the Employee becomes insolvent and unable to pay his or her debts in full or files a petition in bankruptcy or is adjudicated a bankrupt, this agreement shall at once cease and become null and void and the Company shall be under no obligation to the Employee except to pay the Employee such compensation as he or she may be entitled to receive up to the time of such termination.

In the event that the Employee should be arrested or be the subject to an indictment or charged with any crime or unlawful act involving an allegation or charge of a breach of moral turpitude or the sale or use of a prohibited drug or controlled substance, this contract shall at once cease and become null and void and the Company shall be under no obligation to the Employee except to pay the Employee such compensation as he or she may be entitled to receive up to the time of such termination.

In the event that the Employee should be found to have taken, used or converted any property belonging to the Company, the Employee shall be immediately discharged and this contract shall at once cease and become null and void and the Company shall be under no obligation to the Employee except to pay the Employee such compensation as he or she may be entitled to receive up to the time of such termination.

Any payments due the Employee pursuant to termination shall be paid to the Employee as soon as the Company can determine the true and correct amount for all payments due the Employee, except that in the event that said termination is due to the misconduct of the Employee pertaining to any of the terms hereunder, the Company shall have the right to withhold all money due the Employee and shall apply said funds as an offset against any money due the Company from the Employee as a result of the Employee misconduct. In any event, the Employee shall be entitled to an accounting, in writing, of the funds so withheld.

ARTICLE VIII: CONFIDENTIAL INFORMATION. "Confidential Information" shall be defined for the purpose of this agreement as information (1) disclosed to the Employee or known or gathered by the Employee as a consequence of or through his or her employment by the Company and (2) not generally known to the industry in which the Company is or may become engaged about the Company's products, administrative services or methods of doing business, including, but not limited to, information relating to trade secrets, marketing techniques and programs, dates, figures, projections, costs, methods of operation, identity of plans or administrative services, estimates, customer lists, customer history, personnel history, financial statements, accounting procedures and selling techniques.

That the Employee will not during his or her employment or after termination thereof, irrespective of the time, manner or cause of the termination of said employment, directly or indirectly disclose to any person, firm or corporation any of the above Confidential Information that he or she shall have acquired during his or her term of employment.

The Employee agrees that he or she will not, during his or her employment by the Company or at any time thereafter, interfere with or disrupt, or attempt to interfere with or disrupt, any business relationship, contractual or otherwise, between the Company and any other party, including clients or prospective clients, suppliers, agents or the employees of the Company.

The Employee acknowledges that all documents, words, files, customer lists, information and data in his or her possession or custody, whether gathered by the Employee or any other person, and whether or not reduced to writing, an electronic or magnetic medium, relating to the business activities of the Company are and shall remain the sole and exclusive property of the Company and/or the Company's customers.

That upon the termination of said employment, irrespective of the time, manner or cause of said termination, the Employee will surrender to the Company all information written or otherwise in connection with the Company's customers or business as well as other property of the Company.

ARTICLE IX: NONCOMPETITION PROVISION. In further consideration of employment, the Employee shall not engage in a business in any manner similar to or in competition with the Company's or the Company's affiliated businesses during the term of his or her employment. Furthermore, the Employee shall not engage in a business in any manner similar to or in competition with the Company's business for a period of   ( ) years from the date of termination of his or her employment with the Company in the geographical area within a   ( )-mile radius of any present or future office opened by the Company during the term of employment and the geographical area within a   ( )-mile radius of the Employee's home address.

The Employee shall not request any customers of any business then being conducted or contemplated by the Company or its affiliates to curtail or cancel their business with the Company or its affiliates.

The Employee shall not disclose to any person, firm or corporation any trade, technical or technological secrets, any details of organizations or business affairs, any names of past or present customers of the Company or its affiliates or any other information relating to the business or businesses or their affiliates.

The Employee shall not solicit, canvass or accept any business or transaction for any other person, firm or corporation or business similar to any business of the Company or its affiliates.

The Employee shall not induce, or attempt to influence, any employee of the business or its affiliates to terminate employment with the business or its affiliates or to enter into any employment or other business relationship with any other person (including the Employee), firm or corporation.

The Employee shall not act or conduct himself or herself in any manner that he or she shall have reason to believe is inimical or contrary to the best interests of the Company or its affiliates.

The Employee shall not perform any act in violation hereof through any other person or entity or through any plan, scheme or design calculated to circumvent the requirements hereof.

The Employee acknowledges and agrees that the above restriction is reasonable as to duration and geography, that it is fully enforceable, and waives any objection thereto and covenants to institute no suit or proceeding or otherwise advance any position or contention to the contrary.

The Employee recognizes that immediate and irreparable damage will result to the Company if the Employee breaches any of the terms and conditions of this article and, accordingly, the Employee hereby consents to the entry of temporary, preliminary and permanent injunctive relief by any court of competent jurisdiction against him or her to restrain any such breach, in addition to any other remedies or claims for money damages that the Company may seek; and the Employee agrees to render an equitable accounting of all earnings, profits and other benefits arising from such violations; and to pay all costs and counsel fees incurred by the Company in enforcing this agreement, which rights shall be cumulative. The Employee represents and warrants to the Company that his or her experience and capabilities are such that he or she can obtain employment in business without breaching the terms and conditions of this article and that his or her obligations under the provisions of this article (and the enforcement thereof by injunction or otherwise) will not prevent him or her from earning a livelihood.

This covenant on the part of the Employee shall be construed as an agreement independent of any other provisions of this agreement, and the existence of any claim or cause of action of the Employee against the Company, whether predicated on this agreement or otherwise, shall not constitute a defense to the enforcement by the Company of this covenant.

In the event that the Employee is in breach of any of the provisions of this Article IX, the period of proscription from doing the act or acts that constitute a breach of this Article IX shall be extended for a period of two (2) years from the date that the Employee ceased, whether voluntarily or by court order, to engage in or do said actions.

The Employee recognizes and agrees that the Company does not have a remedy at law adequate to protect the Company's rights and interests as set forth in this article, and the Employee therefore agrees that the Company shall have the right to an injunction enjoining the Employee from violating the provisions of this article. Nothing herein contained shall be construed as prohibiting the Company from pursuing any other remedies available to the Company for such breach or threatened breach, including the recovery of damages from the Employee.

If any action at law or equity is necessary to enforce or interpret the terms of this agreement, the Employee agrees to pay the Company reasonable attorney's fees, costs and necessary disbursements, in addition to any other relief and/or damages to which the Company may be entitled.

In the event that a court of competent jurisdiction determines that this restrictive covenant and covenant not to compete is unenforceable in whole or in part for any reason, including, without limitation, the duration, scope and remedies set forth above, then same shall not be void, but rather shall be enforced to the extent that same is deemed to be enforceable by said court, as if originally executed in that form by the parties hereto.

ARTICLE X: MISCELLANEOUS. Service of all notice under this agreement shall be sufficient if made by registered mail to the specific party involved herein at his or her respective address hereinafter set forth or as such party may provide from time to time in writing:

For the Company:

For the Employee:

This agreement constitutes the entire agreement between the parties hereto and supersedes all prior negotiations, understandings and agreements, whether oral or written, of any nature whatsoever with respect to the term of employment that is the subject matter hereof, and there are no representations, warranties, understandings or agreements other than those expressly set forth herein between the Company and the Employee. This agreement cannot be changed, modified or terminated except in writing and signed by the parties hereto.

The validity, interpretation, construction and enforcement of this agreement shall be governed by the laws of the state of   .

The Company shall have the right, but not the obligation, to assign this agreement and the Company's rights hereunder in whole, but not in part, to any corporation or other entity with or into which the Company may hereafter merge or consolidate or to which the Company may transfer all or substantially all of its assets provided such corporation or other entity assumes all of the Company's obligations hereunder.

The Employee understands and acknowledges that his or her employment contract is a contract for personal services of the Employee and cannot be assigned.

This contract is for the personal services of the Employee and shall cease and desist and be considered null and void upon the termination of the contract under any of the provisions hereto.

The invalidity or unenforceability of any particular provision of this agreement shall not affect the other provisions hereto and the agreement shall be construed in all respects as though such invalid or unenforceable provision were omitted.

Any legal action undertaken by the Employee pursuant to any of the terms or conditions or the interpretation thereof shall be commenced within six (6) months of said termination. The Employee agrees hereby that after a term of six (6) months has expired, no legal action against the Company may be brought in any court regarding any term or condition of this agreement.

IN WITNESS WHEREOF, the parties hereto acknowledge, understand and agree to this Employment Agreement. The parties understand and intend to be bound by all of the clauses contained in this document and further certify that they have received signed copies of this agreement.

Company By:

_____

President

_____

Employee

EXPENSE REIMBURSEMENT CONTRACT

_____

Date:

The undersigned officer or shareholder/employee agrees to reimburse

_____ (the Company) for expenses that are deter-

mined by the Internal Revenue Service not to constitute a deductible

business expense pursuant to the Internal Revenue Code of 1986, as

amended. The amount to be repaid shall be an amount equal to that which is

disallowed by the Internal Revenue Service, upon a final determination of

such disallowance.

_____

EXPENSE ACCOUNT REPORT

Employee:

Department:

Expenses authorized by:

Period covered:

Purpose of meal or trip:

Companies or individuals visited:

Specific Expenses

Hotels/Motels: $

Meals: $

Tips: $

Auto Expense:

    Mileage at   ¢ per mile $

    Tolls $

    Parking $

Telephone: $

Miscellaneous: $

Entertainment:* $

    Total Expenses: $

*List persons entertained, nature of entertainment and results of the meeting:

_____

Employee

Reviewed and approved:

_____

Date approved: _____

EMPLOYEE'S CONSENT TO DISCLOSE INFORMATION

Date:

I,   , have been informed that my current employer has been requested to provide information about my employment from

.

I hereby authorize my employer to release the information without
limitation.

_____

NONCOMPETITION CONTRACT

IN CONSIDERATION OF EMPLOYMENT AND OTHER VALUABLE CONSIDERATION that is
acknowledged, the undersigned,   (hereinafter
"Employee") shall not engage in a business in any manner similar to or in
competition with   (hereinafter the
"Company") or the Company's affiliated businesses during the term of
his or her employment. Furthermore, the Employee shall not engage in a
business in any manner similar to or in competition with the Company's
business for a period of   (   ) years from the date of termination of
his or her employment with the Company in the geographical area within a
(   )-mile radius of any present or future office opened by the Company
during the term of employment and the geographical area within a
(   )-mile radius of the Employee's home address.

For the purpose of this agreement, the Employee shall be regarded as
engaging in a "business in any manner similar to or in competition with
the Company's business" if, directly or as an independent contractor or
employee of any business, the Employee is engaged in the business of
                        or such other business or businesses as the
Company is engaged in either individually or as part of some other business entity or affiliate during the term of the Employee's employment by
the Company.

The Employee shall not request any customers of any business then being conducted or contemplated by the Company or its affiliates to curtail or cancel their business with the business or its affiliates.

The Employee shall not disclose to any person, firm or corporation any trade, technical or technological secrets, any details of organizations or business affairs, any names of past or present customers of the Company or its affiliates or any other information relating to the business or businesses or their affiliates.

The Employee shall not solicit, canvass or accept any business or transaction for any other person, firm or corporation or business similar to any business of the Company or its affiliates.

The Employee shall not induce, or attempt to influence, any employee of the Company or its affiliates to terminate employment with the Company or its affiliates or to enter into any employment or other business relationship with any other person (including the Employee), firm or corporation.

The Employee shall not act or conduct himself or herself in any manner that he or she shall have reason to believe is inimical or contrary to the best interests of the Company or its affiliates.

The Employee shall not perform any act in violation hereof through any other person or entity, or through any plan, scheme or design calculated to circumvent the requirements hereof.

The Employee acknowledges and agrees that the above restriction is reasonable as to duration and geography, that it is fully enforceable, and waives any objection thereto and covenants to institute no suit or proceeding or otherwise advance any position or contention to the contrary.

The Employee recognizes that immediate and irreparable damage will result to the Company if the Employee breaches any of the terms and conditions of this agreement and, accordingly, the Employee hereby consents to the entry of temporary, preliminary and permanent injunctive relief by any court of competent jurisdiction against him or her to restrain any such breach, in addition to any other remedies or claims for money damages that the Company may seek; and the Employee agrees to render an equitable accounting of all earnings, profits and other benefits arising from such violations; and to pay all costs and counsel fees incurred by the Company in enforcing this agreement, which rights shall be cumulative.

The Employee represents and warrants to the Company that his or her experience and capabilities are such that he or she can obtain employment in business without breaching the terms and conditions of this agreement and that his or her obligations under the provisions of this agreement (and the enforcement thereof by injunction or otherwise) will not prevent him or her from earning a livelihood.

The existence of any claim or cause of action of the Employee against the Company, whether predicated on this agreement or otherwise, shall not constitute a defense to the enforcement by the Company of this covenant.

In the event that the Employee is in breach of any of the provisions of this agreement as set forth above, the period of proscription from doing the act or acts that constitute a breach of this agreement shall be extended for a period of ( ) years from the date that the Employee ceased, whether voluntarily or by court order, to engage in or do said actions.

The Employee recognizes and agrees that the Company does not have a remedy at law adequate to protect the Company's rights and interests as set forth in this agreement, and the Employee therefore agrees that the Company shall have the right to an injunction enjoining the Employee from violating the provisions of this agreement. Nothing herein contained shall be construed as prohibiting the Company from pursuing any other remedies available to the Company for such breach or threatened breach.

If any action at law or equity is necessary to enforce or interpret the terms of this agreement, the Employee agrees to pay the Company reasonable attorney's fees, costs and necessary disbursements, in addition to any other relief and/or damages to which the Company may be entitled.

In the event that a court of competent jurisdiction determines that this covenant not to compete is unenforceable in whole or in part for any reason, including, without limitation, the duration, scope and remedies set forth above, then same shall not be void, but rather shall be enforced to the extent that same is deemed to be enforceable by said court, as if originally executed in that form by the parties hereto.

Service of all notice under this agreement shall be sufficient if made by registered mail to the specific party involved herein at his or her respective address hereinafter set forth or as such party may provide from time to time in writing:

For the Company:

For the Employee:

This agreement constitutes the entire agreement between the parties hereto and supersedes all prior negotiations, understandings and agreements, whether oral or written, of any nature whatsoever with respect to the term of employment that is the subject matter hereof, and there are no representations, warranties, understandings or agreements other than those expressly set forth herein between the Company and the Employee.

This agreement is not to be changed, modified or terminated except in writing and signed by the parties hereto.

The validity, interpretation, construction and enforcement of this agreement shall be governed by the laws of the state of   .

The invalidity or unenforceability of any particular provision of this agreement shall not affect the other provisions hereto and the agreement shall be construed in all respects as though such invalid or unenforceable provision were omitted.

IN WITNESS WHEREOF, the parties hereto acknowledge, understand and agree to this agreement. The parties understand and intend to be bound by all of the clauses contained in this document and further certify that they have received signed copies of this agreement on this date.

Employee:

_____

For the Company:

_____

(Notary Public)

ACKNOWLEDGMENT

This acknowledgment shall be attached to and considered part of the employment agreement executed this date by and between Company and the Employee,   .

The Employee recognizes, understands and specifically agrees to the (   )-year restrictive covenant contained in the foregoing agreement. The Employee further acknowledges that said   (   )-year restrictive covenant and the geographical limitations set forth therein is reasonable.

I UNDERSTAND AND AGREE THAT I WILL NOT COMPETE IN ANY MANNER AGAINST THE COMPANY, DIRECTLY OR INDIRECTLY FOR A PERIOD OF   (   ) YEARS FROM THE TIME I LEAVE, VOLUNTARILY OR BY TERMINATION, THE EMPLOYMENT OF THE COMPANY.

I understand that my employment with the Company is absolutely conditioned upon execution of this Acknowledgment and agreement. I have fully read, understand and agree to be bound by the attached agreement and this Acknowledgment. I,   , hereby further acknowledge and confirm that I have read and understand the foregoing agreement.

I understand that I have the right and the time to have this agreement reviewed by legal counsel of my choice but decline to do so.

IN WITNESS WHEREOF, and intending to be legally bound hereby, the
Employee has set his or her hand and seal on this   day of   ,
19   , and hereby acknowledges, understands and agrees to the above.

Employee: _____

(Notary Public) _____

NONCOMPETITION CONTRACT
(SHORT FORM)

IN CONSIDERATION OF EMPLOYMENT AND OTHER VALUABLE CONSIDERATION that is acknowledged,   (hereinafter "Employee") shall not for a period of   (   ) years from the date of termination of his or her employment with   (hereinafter "Company") in the geographical area within a   (   )-mile radius of any present or future office opened by the Company during the term of my employment and the geographical area within a   (   )-mile radius of the Employee's home address request any customers of any business then being conducted or contemplated by the Company or its affiliates to curtail or cancel their business with the Company or its affiliates.

The Employee acknowledges and agrees that the above restriction is reasonable as to duration and geography, that it is fully enforceable, and waives any objection thereto and covenants to institute no suit or proceeding or otherwise advance any position or contention to the contrary.

The Employee recognizes that immediate and irreparable damage will result to the Company if the Employee breaches any of the terms and conditions of this agreement and, accordingly, the Employee hereby consents to the entry of temporary, preliminary and permanent injunctive relief by any court of competent jurisdiction against him or her to restrain any such breach, in addition to any other remedies or claims for money damages that the Company may seek; and the Employee agrees to render an equitable accounting of all earnings, profits and other benefits arising from such violations; and to pay all costs and counsel fees incurred by the Company in enforcing this agreement, which rights shall be cumulative. The Employee represents and warrants to the Company that his or her experience and capabilities are such that he or she can obtain employment in business without breaching the terms and conditions of this agreement and that his or her obligations under the provisions of this paragraph (and the enforcement thereof by injunction or otherwise) will not prevent him or her from earning a livelihood.

In the event that a court of competent jurisdiction determines that this restrictive covenant and covenant not to compete is unenforceable in whole or in part for any reason, including, without limitation, the duration, scope and remedies set forth above, then same shall not be void, but rather shall be enforced to the extent that same is deemed to be enforceable by said court, as if originally executed in that form by the parties hereto.

Service of all notice under this agreement shall be sufficient if made by registered mail to the specific party involved herein at his or her respective address hereinafter set forth or as such party may provide from time to time in writing:

For the Company:

For the Employee:

This agreement constitutes the entire agreement between the parties hereto and supersedes all prior negotiations, understandings and agreements, whether oral or written, of any nature whatsoever with respect to the term of employment that is the subject matter hereof, and there are no representations, warranties, understandings or agreements other than those expressly set forth herein between the Company and the Employee.

This agreement cannot be changed, modified or terminated except in writing and signed by the parties hereto.

The validity, interpretation, construction and enforcement of this agreement shall be governed by the laws of the state of   .

_____

(*Notary Public*)

NONCOMPETITION CONTRACT
(Limiting Geographic Areas of Competition)

IN CONSIDERATION OF EMPLOYMENT AND OTHER VALUABLE CONSIDERATION that is acknowledged, _____ (hereinafter "Employee") shall not engage in a business in any manner similar to or in competition with _____ (hereinafter "Company") or the Company's affiliated businesses during the term of his or her employment.

Furthermore, the Employee shall not engage in a business in any manner similar to or in competition with the Company's business in the geographical area within a ( )-mile radius of any present or future office opened by the Company during the term of employment and the geographical area within a ( )-mile radius of the Employee's home address.

For the purpose of this agreement, the Employee shall be regarded as engaging in a "business in any manner similar to or in competition with the Company's business" if, directly or as an independent contractor or employee of any business, the Employee is engaged in the business of _____ or such other business or businesses as the Company is engaged in either individually or as part of some other business entity or affiliate.

The Employee acknowledges and agrees that the above restriction is reasonable as to duration and geography, that it is fully enforceable, and waives any objection thereto and covenants to institute no suit or proceeding or otherwise advance any position or contention to the contrary.

The Employee recognizes that immediate and irreparable damage will result to the Company if the Employee breaches any of the terms and conditions of this agreement and, accordingly, the Employee hereby consents to the entry of temporary, preliminary and permanent injunctive relief by any court of competent jurisdiction against him or her to restrain any such breach, in addition to any other remedies or claims for money damages that the Company may seek; and the Employee agrees to render an equitable accounting of all earnings, profits and other benefits arising from such violations; and to pay all costs and counsel fees incurred by the Company in enforcing this agreement, which rights shall be cumulative.

The existence of any claim or cause of action of the Employee against the Company, whether predicated on this agreement or otherwise, shall not constitute a defense to the enforcement by the Company of this covenant.

If any action at law or equity is necessary to enforce or interpret the terms of this agreement, the Employee agrees to pay the Company reasonable attorney's fees, costs and necessary disbursements, in addition to any other relief and/or damages to which the Company may be entitled.

In the event that a court of competent jurisdiction determines that this restrictive covenant and covenant not to compete is unenforceable in whole or in part for any reason, including, without limitation, the scope and remedies set forth above, then same shall not be void, but rather shall be enforced to the extent that same is deemed to be enforceable by said court, as if originally executed in that form by the parties hereto.

Service of all notice under this agreement shall be sufficient if made by registered mail to the specific party involved herein at his or her respective address hereinafter set forth or as such party may provide from time to time in writing:

For the Company:

For the Employee:

This agreement constitutes the entire agreement between the parties hereto and supersedes all prior negotiations, understandings and agreements, whether oral or written, of any nature whatsoever with respect to the term of employment that is the subject matter hereof, and there are no representations, warranties, understandings or agreements other than those expressly set forth herein between the Company and the Employee.

This agreement cannot be changed, modified or terminated except in writing and signed by the parties hereto.

_____

(*Notary Public*)

NOTICE OF WORK-PERFORMANCE DEFICIENCIES

Date:

To:

This letter confirms our recent meeting of   , 19   , when we

discussed your poor job performance. You were cautioned that your perform-

ance was not acceptable in the following respects:

Based on the above factors, you have been given an unsatisfactory per-

formance rating. For you to enjoy a good status standing, you must improve

your performance and, as we discussed, adopt the following action plan to

improve your performance:

We trust that this notice is accepted as constructive and that we can

look forward to improved performance on your part.

As you will note, a copy of this notice has been attached. Please sign

that copy where indicated and return it to me promptly.

Sincerely,

_____

Receipt acknowledged: _____

FINAL DISMISSAL NOTICE

Date:

To:

You have been counseled and warned of deficiencies in your job performance (see notification dated   , 19   , a copy of which is attached).

Regretfully, the deficiencies do not seem to have been corrected. Immediate action, in conformity with the earlier notification mentioned above, must be taken by you to correct your performance deficiencies. I cannot stress too strongly that such action must be undertaken without delay. Failure to comply will result in your dismissal without additional notice.

I have attached a copy of this notice; please sign where indicated and return the copy to me promptly.

_____

Receipt acknowledged: _____

                      Employee

DISMISSAL NOTIFICATION

Date:

To:

This memorandum confirms the conversation we had earlier on   ,

19   , during which you were advised that your services for the company

will not be required after   , 19   , and that your employment

with the company will terminate on that date.

This action was taken for the following reason(s):

Severance pay and accrued benefits shall continue pursuant to the

company's specific benefit program and in conformity with the law. Please

make an appointment with   , so that we may

discuss the termination procedure and your right to benefits.

I have attached a copy of this notice; please sign the copy where

indicated and promptly return the copy to me.

We wish you well in your future endeavors.

Sincerely,

_____

Receipt acknowledged: _____

Employee

6

Buying and Selling Goods

Introduction

Most daily business transactions are governed by Article 2 of the UCC. This article is so extensive that it may even add terms to a contract where the contract is silent on those terms. This chapter provides forms that will protect your rights under the UCC and preserve any remedies that you may have if the other party breaches a contract.

The Initial Order

All of the forms in this chapter should be prepared on your business stationery. Form 601 asks a supplier for a firm price on goods that you wish to purchase. This form will obligate a supplier, in the event you purchase, to the prices the supplier has submitted. Form 602 can be used by a supplier to inform a customer that goods ordered by the customer will be shipped cash on delivery (COD). If the supplier does not supply this information, the buyer may have the right to expect that he or she will be billed after delivery.

Form 603 should be used by the buyer to confirm a telephone order; by using it, you will avoid any misunderstanding regarding quality, quantity, price, credit and delivery terms. Form 604 is the seller's version of Form 603 and serves the same purpose as that form. Form 605 should be used in place of Form 604 if the buyer's entire order will be filled with more than one shipment.

Form 606 is designed for sellers who have received orders without shipping instructions. If a buyer does not respond to the seller's request for shipping instructions, the seller is not obliged to ship the order. Form 607 notifies the purchaser that the goods are being held and supplies a checklist of reasons for the seller's decision not to ship.

Forms 608 and 609 should be used for approval or consignment sales. Each form sets out the terms of the transaction. Should the purchaser return goods accepted on approval (Form 608), he or she should use Form 610 to return the goods.

Delivery and Cancellation

In Form 611, the buyer acknowledges that the goods he or she purchased were received and are acceptable. Before issuing this receipt you must ensure that you have had adequate time to carefully inspect the goods. If the goods later turn out to be faulty in some respect, the receipt you issued may weaken any claim you may have against the supplier.

Form 612 should be used when the parties agree to amend the terms of the purchase contract. The buyer or seller who initiates this form should mail two signed copies of the form so that the other party can return a signed copy. Suppliers can use Form 613 to notify their customers of delivery dates. There is no legal requirement calling for a shipping notice; however, it does help to promote good relationships.

Form 614 can be used by a buyer to cancel items that the supplier has put on back order. This right is provided to buyers by the UCC, but you must exercise it promptly.

Forms 615 and 616 deal with the delivery of goods. Failure to make delivery pursuant to the purchase contract is generally considered a breach of the contract. Form 615 should be used when the buyer has made payment. Form 616 should be used by the buyer to ask the seller to supply delivery dates, and it retains the buyer's right to cancel the order if the seller does not supply a delivery date.

Form 617 adopts a checklist format that buyers can use to reject goods that were delivered. The UCC provides the purchaser with remedies for nonconforming items. The primary remedy is rejection, which you may use to reject all or a part of the shipment.

Forms 618 through 620 deals with damaged goods. The purchaser has the option under the UCC to reject or retain the goods. Form 618 assumes the buyer will accept the damaged goods, but wants an allowance on the price. If the seller does not agree to a reduced price, the buyer still retains the right to reject the goods.

In Form 619, the buyer rejects the shipment and asks the seller for return shipping instructions. Buyers who have prepaid for the shipment should use Form 620.

In the event that goods are not delivered in a timely fashion, the buyer can use Form 621 to cancel the order.

A seller who has received notice that the buyer will not or has not accepted delivery can use Form 622 to respond to the buyer and preserve the seller's rights against the buyer for a breach of contract.

Form 623 is a notice of resale. One remedy the UCC provides to suppliers is to permit the seller to sell items in question and then to look to the buyer for any deficiency between the sale and the contract price.

Form 624 can be used by a seller to advise a shipping company to stop the shipment of goods. Unless a "Negotiable Bill of Lading" has been given to the purchaser, the seller has an absolute right to stop a shipment.

Return and Disputes

If your customer becomes insolvent within ten days of the date that he or she received a shipment from you, the UCC gives you the right to demand a return of the goods included in the shipment. Form 625 should be used by suppliers to demand that insolvent customers return delivered goods.

Form 626 should be used by purchasers to notify their suppliers of a disagreement regarding their outstanding account balance. Purchasers should be careful to monitor their bills, because a failure to challenge the amounts set out in your bills may act as an admission of the amounts claimed by the supplier. Form 627 should be used by a purchaser whenever a dispute about the account balance exists. Even if the check you send states that it is in payment of specific invoices, you still should use this form to direct your creditor to apply the payment to specified, undisputed accounts.

BID REQUEST

_____

Date:

To:

Kindly provide us with your bid for the following items:

Item	Quantity	Unit Price	Total Price
_____	_____	$ _____	$ _____
_____	_____	$ _____	$ _____
_____	_____	$ _____	$ _____
_____	_____	$ _____	$ _____
_____	_____	$ _____	$ _____
_____	_____	$ _____	$ _____

Please quote your bid delivery to us free on board (FOB) at the following location:

If your bid prices will not remain firm for at least thirty (30) days, please advise us of when the bid price no longer will be effective.

Sincerely,

_____

NOTICE THAT SALE WILL BE ON COD TERMS

Date:

To:

We welcome your patronage and acknowledge receipt of your order for goods.
With respect to payment terms, please be advised that we will ship your
order cash on delivery (COD) ten (10) days from the date of this letter,
unless you cancel the order or make other financing arrangements within
the next ten (10) days.

Thank you for your order; we hope we can continue to be of service
to you.

Sincerely,

ORDER CONFIRMATION

_____

Date:

To:

Dear   :

This will confirm our order of   ,19   , which we placed with

you by telephone. A purchase order authorizing the order on the terms that

we discussed is attached to this letter.

  If any of the terms set out in the purchase order no longer are accept-

able to you, please advise us within ten (10) days of the date of this

letter; otherwise, we shall deem the order accepted in due form and we

will anticipate prompt delivery.

                    Sincerely,

                    _____

ACCEPTANCE OF AN ORDER

_____

Date:

To:

Dear   :

Receipt of your purchase order number   is hereby acknowledged.

   This will confirm that we have accepted your order with the following

exceptions:

   Unless we receive written notice from you within   (   ) days, we

shall assume that you have accepted our exceptions and we will fulfill the

order according to the above exceptions.

   Your business is greatly appreciated. Thank you.

            Sincerely,

            _____

ACCEPTANCE OF AN ORDER (SHIPMENT IN MORE THAN ONE LOT)

_____

Date:

To:

Dear   :

Receipt of your purchase order dated   , 19   , is hereby

noticed. The items that you ordered will be shipped in the following

different lots:

Payment will be due for each lot as it is delivered.

Sincerely,

_____

REQUEST FOR SHIPPING INSTRUCTIONS

_____

Date:

To:

Dear   :

Your order is important to us. Although we are prepared to fulfill it

promptly, you have not provided delivery instructions.

Kindly provide such directions by return mail, or we shall have to hold

your order.

Sincerely,

_____

NOTIFICATION OF NONSHIPMENT

_____

Date:

To:

Dear   :

We are holding shipment of your order dated   , 19   , for the

following reason(s):

    [ ] Nonpayment.

    [ ] No shipping directions provided.

    [ ] Your contract has been canceled.

    [ ] The following items are on back order:

  [ ] Other:

            Sincerely,

            _____

SALE SUBJECT TO APPROVAL

_____

Date:

To:

Dear   :

Thank you for your order of   . Your request for deliv-

ery of goods on an approval basis is hereby accepted. You have the right

to return the items shipped under the attached invoice within   (   )

days of delivery. Any items not so returned will be considered accepted.

We look forward to doing additional business with you in the future.

Sincerely,

_____

CONSIGNMENT SALE

_____

Date:

To:

Dear   :

In accordance with your invoice (copy attached), we are shipping the goods you ordered on a consignment basis. Any goods not sold by you may be returned to us for credit. If any such goods are returned, you shall be responsible for the cost of shipping those goods to us.

This consignment agreement also includes the following terms:

1. We retain the right to the immediate return of any unsold goods.

2. You have agreed to sign any financing agreements that are needed to protect our ownership rights.

3. All items that you sell under this consignment are subject to the payment terms set out in the attached invoice.

Please indicate that you have accepted the terms of this consignment agreement by signing below under the words "Agreed to and accepted" and returning a signed copy to me by return mail.

Sincerely,

_____

Agreed to and accepted:

_____

NOTICE: RETURN OF APPROVAL-SALE PRODUCTS

_____

Date:

To:

Dear   :

We are returning to you the following goods that you delivered to us on

approval on   , 19   .

   The returned items are:

   We thank you for the opportunity to review your goods.

                    Sincerely,

                    _____

RECEIPT FOR DELIVERY OF GOODS

_____

Date:

To:

Dear   :

We hereby acknowledge that the items listed on the attached form have been

received by us, inspected by us and are accepted by us as in good form

without defect.

Sincerely,

_____

MODIFICATION OF A CONTRACT

_____

Date:

To:

Dear   :

This letter will serve as the written modification of our contract dated

, 19   . The contract is revised as follows:

If the above comports with your understanding of our agreement to

modify our contract, please sign below under the words "Agreed to and

accepted" and return a signed copy of this letter to us at the address

shown above.

Sincerely,

_____

Agreed to and accepted:

_____

SHIPPING NOTICE

_____

Date:

To:

Dear   :

We shipped the items you ordered (see your purchase order numbered

) on   , 19   . You can expect your order to arrive at

your offices on   , 19   .

   Your business is greatly appreciated.

                        Sincerely,

                    _____

NOTICE OF CANCELLATION: BACK-ORDERED ITEMS

_____

Date:

To:

Dear   :

You have notified us that certain items on our purchase order, number

            , dated   , 19   , are not in your stock and have been

back ordered.

Because timely receipt of the items is a necessity for us, please

cancel the back-ordered items from our order and ship the remainder of the

order immediately. Please ensure that the invoice you send to us reflects

the fact that we have canceled the order for the items you have on back

order.

Sincerely,

_____

DEMAND FOR DELIVERY AFTER PAYMENT

_____

Date:

To:

Dear   :

We acted in good faith and have paid   dollars

($), the full purchase price of the items that we ordered from

your firm on   , 19   . Payment was made on   , 19   .

    To date, however, we have not received delivery.

    We hereby demand immediate delivery.

                        Sincerely,

                        _____

DEMAND FOR SHIPPING DATES

_____

Date:

To:

Dear   :

Pursuant to our contract dated   , 19   , we require you to

provide us with the arrangements that you have made to ship the goods that

we ordered to us and that you also provide adequate security that you will

conform to those arrangements.

Should you be unable to provide such information and security, you will

be in violation of the above-described contract and we may choose to termi-

nate it pursuant to its terms.

Sincerely,

_____

NOTICE: REJECTION OF SHIPMENT

_____

Date:

To:

Dear   :

We are in receipt of the items that you shipped to us on   ,

19   . The items are rejected for the following reasons:

[ ]   The items were delivered in damaged condition (see explanation

      attached).

[ ]   The items delivered are defective (see attached explanation).

[ ]   The shipment was not timely delivered.

[ ]   The items were not in compliance with the purchase order (see

      attached explanation).

[ ]   The prices on your invoice are not in compliance with the purchase

      order accepted by your firm.

[ ]   The entire order was not shipped; no back orders are acceptable.

[ ]   Other:

This rejection does not act to limit or waiver any other legal right

that we may have.

Because this order was prepaid, we demand that you issue a credit for the full amount paid to your company.

Sincerely,

_____

NOTICE: ACCEPTANCE OF DAMAGED GOODS

_____

Date:

To:

Dear   :

We are in receipt of certain items pursuant to our purchase order dated

_____ , 19   . The following items arrived damaged or defective in

the following respects:

Pursuant to our conversation, we have agreed to accept said items

subject to an adjustment of   dollars ($)

in the purchase price. Kindly issue a new invoice showing the adjustment

and correct our account accordingly.

Sincerely,

_____

NOTICE: RECEIPT OF DEFECTIVE GOODS

_____

Date:

To:

Dear   :

We have received the items that we ordered from you. However, the follow-

ing items are defective for the reasons listed:

The defective goods are hereby rejected.

We will be making arrangements to ship the defective items back to you

at your expense; please advise us if you have a preference for the form of

shipment or for a specific carrier.

Kindly adjust our account accordingly and provide directions for return-

ing the defective items.

Sincerely,

_____

NOTICE OF NONCONFORMING ITEMS

Date:

To:

Dear   :

We have received the items that you shipped to us on   , 19   ,

pursuant to our purchase order numbered   .

The items you shipped are rejected because they fail to correspond to

our specifications in the following respects:

Because we prepaid for the above-described items, we hereby demand that

you issue a corresponding credit to us promptly. This rejection does not

limit or waiver any other legal right that we may have.

We are preparing to make arrangements to return the above-described

items to your offices at your expense. If you have a preference for the

form of shipment or for a specific carrier, please notify us within the

next   (   ) days.

Sincerely,

NOTICE OF CANCELLATION: FAILURE OF TIMELY DELIVERY

_____

Date:

To:

Dear   :

You have failed to deliver the items that we ordered by purchase order

number   . They were required to be received by us on or before

        , 19   .

Because we have not received these items in a timely manner, pursuant

to our contract, we hereby cancel the order in its entirety.

Sincerely,

_____

SUPPLIER'S RESPONSE TO NONACCEPTANCE

Date:

To:

Dear   :

We acknowledge that you have refused to accept delivery of the items that

you ordered. Accordingly, we shall restock the items in our inventory.

However, we reserve the right to proceed against you for your breach of

contract for all foreseeable and resulting damages.

Sincerely,

NOTICE OF RESALE BY SELLER

_____

Date:

To:

Dear   :

As you have breached the contract dated   , 19   , which you

made with us, this letter is written to inform you that the items that you

ordered will be sold on   , 19   .

    The items will be sold to the highest bidder. If the purchase price at

the sale is less than the price set out in the above-described contract,

you will be required to satisfy any shortfall.

                Sincerely,

            _____

STOP SHIPMENT ORDER

_____

Date:

To:

Dear   :

You are in the process of transporting products for us to the following

addressee: . The shipping order for that

delivery is enclosed.

   We hereby direct you to not deliver said items and return them to us.

We shall pay for the shipping charges. No transfer of title has

occurred, nor is the customer in receipt of any bill of lading.

Sincerely,

_____

(Customer)

CC:

RETURN DEMAND

_____

                          Date:

To:

Dear   :

We have been advised that your firm is insolvent. Accordingly, we demand

that the products that you received from us in the past two weeks be

returned to us immediately.

      According to our records, you have received the following shipments

from us during the past two weeks:

                          Sincerely,

                          _____

CHALLENGE TO ACCOUNT BALANCE

_____

Date:

To:

Dear   :

Your invoice statement shows that we have an outstanding balance of

                 dollars ($). That amount is incorrect

for the following reason(s):

    [ ] The items billed have not been received.

    [ ] The account does not reflect the following payment(s):

    [ ] The account does not reflect the following credit due for returns:

    [ ] The account does not reflect credit due for damaged items.

    [ ] The prices charged are not in conformity with our contract dated

         , 19   .

Kindly adjust our balance accordingly.

                              Sincerely,

                    _____

NOTICE: DIRECTING PAYMENT FOR NAMED ACCOUNTS

_____

Date:

To:

Dear   :

The enclosed payment in the amount of   dollars

($) is to be allocated to the following outstanding invoices

exclusively:

    Invoice Number   Amount

Sincerely,

_____

7

Protecting Copyrights, Inventions, Trade Secrets and Other Intangibles

Introduction

You or your company may have certain intangible assets that far outweigh in value any fixed assets to which they attach. For example, a customer list may be a company's most valued asset. Or if your company is involved in research and development, you may assume any invention or new product that your research workers develop belongs to the company. Similarly, you may have a copyright that is far more valuable than any specific product that you sell. The forms in this chapter are designed to protect your "intangible" assets.

Using Your Forms

One of the most common ways to promote a product is to rely on the testimonial of a respected or well-known person. Before you can use that testimonial, you must have the person's permission. Form 701 can be used to obtain permission from an individual to use both his or her words and picture.

On occasion, you may want to use material copyrighted by someone else as part of a book you are writing or perhaps in conjunction with sales literature. Or someone else may want to use your copyrighted material in his or her work. Form 702 can be used to obtain or provide such permission. Note, however, that it identifies the specific material that can be used and calls for the user to supply the original source with credit in the republication of the copyrighted material. Without that credit line, the copyright holder's right to the exclusive use of the copyrighted material may be jeopardized.

Form 703 should be used by employers to protect their ownership rights to any invention or new product that an employee creates on the employer's time, at the employer's place of business, or which is based on work performed for the employer. We suggest you have the form notarized. This will accomplish two purposes. First, it ensures that the employee knows you take this agreement very seriously. Second, it will bar the employee from claiming that he or she never signed the agreement.

Form 704 should be used whenever your company receives an unsolicited idea, a proposal for a product or a product promotion. The newspapers are filled with articles reporting claims by inventors, writers, even photographers that they are owed money by companies that "used" their ideas. This form sets out the terms on which you will review the proposal. You should send two copies of the form to the person making the proposal and require a signed, notarized copy to be returned to you.

Business Tip

Avoid reading any proposal your company may receive until you receive a notarized copy of Form 704 from the person making the proposal. As soon as it becomes clear to you that a letter contains a proposal, stop reading the letter, place it in a sealed envelope and file it in your company safe or some other secure location. Immediately write a file memorandum setting out how you handled the matter. If your company receives such proposals on even a periodic basis, you may want to establish a written company policy describing how such proposals are to be handled. That policy statement should be disseminated to any employee who might receive proposals from outsiders.

Form 705 is a confidentiality agreement that you should require employees to sign if they will have access to any material that you consider secret. Such information can include, but is not limited to, customer lists, product-development information, technical or manufacturing processes, pricing formulas or marketing plans. Again, we suggest that you have this form notarized, even though that step is not necessary to the enforcement of this form.

AUTHORIZATION TO USE QUOTATION

Date:

FOR GOOD AND VALUABLE CONSIDERATION, receipt of which is acknowledged, I

irrevocably grant permission to   , its

successors and assigns, to utilize the attached statement or picture in

a publication entitled   and any subsequent

editions of that publication, and in connection with the advertising or

promotion of that publication or new editions of that publication.

_____

AUTHORIZATION TO USE COPYRIGHTED MATERIALS

Date:

FOR GOOD AND VALUABLE CONSIDERATION RECEIVED, I, the owner of the copy-

right, authorize   to publish and reprint the

following material:

This grant of permission is strictly limited to the use of the above-

described material in connection with the following publication:

This grant of permission is further conditioned on the agreement of

                                    to credit the undersigned as the author of

the above-described material with a credit line that shall read as follows:

_____

INVENTION AGREEMENT BINDING EMPLOYEE

IN CONSIDERATION of being employed by   (here-

inafter "Company"), I,   , intending to be

legally bound, agree as follows:

1. While employed, I will inform the Company of any inventions,

    improvements or refinements for processes or equipment that:

    (a) Came about as a result of my employment with the Company or as

        a result of any research ideas discussed between myself and

        any other Company employee.

    (b) Came about while using the Company's equipment and plant, or

        on Company time or in conjunction with any other Company em-

        ployee.

    (c) Are related to any aspect of or line of business of the Com-

        pany's business, either currently operating or currently being

        planned.

2. I hereby convey and relinquish to the Company all right and title

    to any of the inventions, improvements or refinements subject to

    paragraph 1 above, which I may create.

3. I will sign and execute any document required by the Company to

    register, perfect and protect any patent that may come about by my

    efforts on behalf of the Company.

4. This agreement shall continue in force after I have left the employ of the Company.

_____

(*Notary Public*)

RESPONSE TO UNSOLICITED IDEAS

_____

Date:

To:

Dear   :

Your submission of a proposal regarding   has

been received by our company. As you may imagine, our firm is the recipi-

ent of many such submissions. Your proposed submission may, in fact,

already have been submitted or considered.

We have not reviewed your proposal and will review it only if you agree

to the following conditions:

1. Submissions, in whole or part, will be returned only if you prepay

    shipping expenses.

2. You will not hold the company responsible for any loss or damage

    to any samples that you submit.

3. The company is not required to maintain confidentiality with

    respect to any portion of your submission.

4. The company will compensate you for your submission only on the

    condition that we mutually agree on all terms.

If the terms and conditions set out above are satisfactory to you and

you wish us to review your submission under those terms and conditions, please sign below under the words "Agreed to and accepted" and return the enclosed signed copy of this letter to us at the address shown above.

Sincerely,

_____

Agreed to and accepted:

_____

CONFIDENTIALITY AGREEMENT

FOR GOOD AND VALUABLE CONSIDERATION, receipt of which is acknowledged, and further consideration of employment with   ,

I hereby acknowledge the facts set out below and agree to be bound as follows:

1. I acknowledge that during the tenure of my employment, I may come in possession of company information that the company deems to be a trade secret. Such information may be either business related, i.e., customer lists and confidential product price lists, or technically related to the company's business, i.e., engineering procedures, computer programming or research information.

2. I will not during my tenure with the company and for a period of   (   ) years after I leave my employment with the company disclose to any person, company, corporation, partnership or other entity, nor use on my own, nor in conjunction with any other person, company, corporation, partnership or other entity any trade secrets of the company.

3. When my tenure of employment with the company ends, I will promptly return to the appropriate company officers all the documents of the company that are in my possession. Furthermore, I represent and warrant that I will not improperly maintain copies of any such records.

4. The company maintains the right to proceed against me for injunctive relief, should I violate the provisions of any of the above paragraphs.

5. This agreement is for the benefit of the company and shall remain in full force and effect on my heirs and successors. Furthermore, the company may transfer or assign this agreement without my consent.

_____
(Notary Public)

Assignments

Introduction

Most business property will be sold or transferred by an assignment at one time or another. Under the laws of most states, an assignment must be in written form. This chapter will provide the forms that you will need to sell or assign virtually any form of personal property in which you own an interest. For our purposes, the term *personal property* refers to any property other than an interest in real estate.

Assigning Income and Accounts Receivable

Form 801 is a general form of assignment. When you use it, remember to fully describe the property being transferred.

Form 802 assigns income to be earned or received by the assigning party (assignor). This assignment must be given to the employer or client (if the assignor is an independent contractor) who will be paying money to the assignor.

Form 803 assigns the right to collect and receive the proceeds of a businessperson's accounts receivable. If you will be the purchaser of these accounts, make sure that you are purchasing them with recourse. When you take them with recourse, you retain the right to pursue the company or person from whom you purchased the accounts in the event that you are unsuccessful in collecting on one or more of the accounts. Form 804 is an assignment without recourse. Using this form of assignment places you at greater risk (if you are buying the accounts) than if you use Form 803.

Forms 805 through 807 require both the assigning party and the receiving party to sign the agreement. Form 805 can be used when a contract is to be assigned. Form 806 should be used when a security interest is to be assigned. If you wish to assign any type of damage claim, Form 807 should be used. Form 808 is designed for use when a stock certificate will be assigned and the signature should be guaranteed by a bank or if you are a smaller corporation by a notary public.

If you are taking an assignment from someone who is owed a debt, make sure that you use Form 809 to notify the debtor that the amount owed will be paid to you.

Assigning Intangibles

Form 810 assigns the right to literary property for which a copyright has not been obtained. Form 811 assigns the right to copyrighted material. Form 812 can be used to assign a trademark. This assignment also should be registered with the United States Patent Office using assignment forms required by and available at the patent office.

ASSIGNMENT

FOR GOOD AND VALUABLE CONSIDERATION, receipt of which is acknowledged,

I/we hereby convey and assign to   all my/our

ownership rights and interest in the following:

Dated: _____

                              _____

INCOME ASSIGNMENT

Date:

FOR GOOD AND VALUABLE CONSIDERATION, receipt of which is acknowledged,

I/we hereby convey and assign to   all my/our

rights and interest in the proceeds and funds of a certain contract by and

between myself/ourselves and   , dated

    , 19   .

_____

_____

RECEIVABLES ASSIGNMENT

Date:

FOR GOOD AND VALUABLE CONSIDERATION, receipt of which is acknowledged,

I/we hereby convey and assign to

("Assignee") all my/our ownership rights and interest in the following

accounts receivables:

This transfer is made pursuant to a contract between myself/ourselves

and the Assignee dated   , 19   .

I/we acknowledge that if any of the accounts transferred shall be

uncollectible in part or in whole, that my/our account shall be adjusted

accordingly.

_____

_____

NONRECOURSE RECEIVABLES ASSIGNMENT

Date:

FOR GOOD AND VALUABLE CONSIDERATION, receipt of which is acknowledged,

I/we hereby convey and assign to

("Assignee") all my/our ownership rights and interest in the following

accounts receivables:

This transfer is made pursuant to a contract between myself/ourselves

and the Assignee dated   , 19   . The Assignee acknowledges that

said assignment is in satisfaction of the outstanding debt and that said

transfer is without recourse for nonpayment.

_____

Assignor

_____

Assignee

CONTRACT ASSIGNMENT

FOR GOOD AND VALUABLE CONSIDERATION, receipt of which is acknowledged, I/we hereby convey and assign to

("Assignee") all my/our ownership rights and interest in the following contract:

The assignor(s) represents that the contract is assignable, that it is not for personal services and that it has not been terminated.

The Assignee shall perform all of the duties of the assignor(s) pursuant to the contract and shall indemnify the assignor(s) from any and all claims arising out of the contract.

Date: _____

_____

Assignor

_____

Assignee

SECURITY ASSIGNMENT AGREEMENT

Date:

FOR GOOD AND VALUABLE CONSIDERATION, receipt of which is acknowledged,

I/we hereby convey and assign to

("Assignee") all my/our ownership rights and interest in the following

security agreements:

The assignor represents that the security interest is assignable and that it has not been terminated.

The Assignee shall perform all of the duties of the assignor pursuant to the security agreement and shall indemnify the assignor from any and all claims arising out of the security agreement. Furthermore, the assignor shall provide reasonable notification to the debtor regarding this assignment.

_____

Assignor

_____

Assignee

DAMAGE CLAIM ASSIGNMENT

Date:

FOR GOOD AND VALUABLE CONSIDERATION, receipt of which is acknowledged,

I/we hereby convey and assign to

("Assignee") all my/our ownership rights and interest of any type in the

following claim:

The assignor represents that the claim is assignable and that it has

not been settled. Furthermore, the assignor agrees to provide all reason-

able assistance to the Assignee in pursuing the above-described claim.

_____

Assignor

_____

Assignee

STOCK CERTIFICATE ASSIGNMENT

Date:

FOR GOOD AND VALUABLE CONSIDERATION, receipt of which is acknowledged,

I/we hereby convey and assign to

("Assignee") all my/our ownership rights and interest of any type what-

soever in the shares of stock of the

Corporation, which are represented by share certificates numbered

and attached hereto.

    I hereby nominate   as my attorney-in-fact

and authorize him or her to transfer the above-described shares on the

stock ledger of the above-mentioned corporation.

_____

Assignor

(Notary Public or bank verification)

NOTIFICATION OF DEBT ASSIGNMENT

Date:

To:

Dear   :

Your creditor,   , has conveyed your account

to us. To guarantee that you receive proper credit, all future payments

should be sent directly to us at the following address:

Furthermore, kindly confirm that your outstanding balance is

dollars ($).

Sincerely,

_____

LITERARY MATERIAL ASSIGNMENT

Date:

FOR GOOD AND VALUABLE CONSIDERATION, receipt of which is acknowledged,

I/we hereby convey and assign to

("Assignee") all my/our ownership rights and interest in the following

literary material:

The Assignee may apply for copyrights on the material and utilize them

as the owner of the same.

—————————————

COPYRIGHT ASSIGNMENT

Date:

FOR GOOD AND VALUABLE CONSIDERATION, receipt of which is acknowledged,

I/we hereby convey and assign to

("Assignee") all my/our ownership rights and interest in the following

copyright:

The copyright certification is attached as Exhibit "A."

The assignor represents that he or she owns clear and marketable title

to the above-described copyright and knows of no outstanding claims

against the copyright.

_____

TRADEMARK ASSIGNMENT

Date:

FOR GOOD AND VALUABLE CONSIDERATION, receipt of which is acknowledged,

I/we hereby convey and assign to

("Assignee") all my/our ownership rights and interest in the following

trademark:

The trademark certification is attached as Exhibit "A."

The assignor represents that he or she owns clear and marketable title

to the above-described trademark and knows of no outstanding claims

against the trademark.

_____

9

Miscellaneous Forms

The forms in this chapter relate to a variety of transactions. For example, there are forms for specialized sales agreements, various types of releases and corporate transactions.

Specialized Sales and Business Agreements

Form 901 is a conditional sales agreement. In this type of transaction, the "buyer" does not actually receive title until he or she has made the last payment to the seller. Because the goods are delivered to the buyer, a stranger might well believe that the goods belong to the buyer and might either purchase them or extend credit using the goods as collateral. To avoid this, the UCC protects the seller by permitting him or her to file a copy of the conditional sales agreement at the local filing office in the county where the goods will be located. The instructions on Form 901 remind you to file with your local authorities (if you are in doubt as to the proper place to file, check with your county courthouse).

Form 902 is a consignment agreement. As is the case with a conditional sale, consigned goods are delivered to a "buyer" (the consignee) who, in effect, is really only an agent for the seller. Nevertheless, the goods are in the "buyer's" hands and potential customers or lenders may be misled into thinking the consignee is the rightful owner of the goods. Again, the UCC protects the seller/consignor if he or she files the consignment agreement with the proper authorities in the county in which the consignee and the goods are located. Form 902 contains a reminder advising you to file the completed form with the appropriate local authority.

Form 903 is an indemnification agreement that can be used for any situation in which one person agrees to indemnify the other. Note that you must identify the liability for which the indemnification is being offered. If you are to provide the indemnity, make sure that you word the description as narrowly and accurately as possible—you do not want the indemnity to go beyond what you intend to protect against. If the indemnity is being offered to you, you should be equally careful; you do not want the description to be so narrow that it does not include matters that cause you concern. Although it is not required by law, prudence suggests that it is wise to have the person who is making the indemnification promise have his or her signature notarized.

Form 904 is the stock purchase agreement that you can use when your corporation sells shares of its stock to a new investor.

Form 905 is the noncompetition agreement that can be used if your business relies on independent contractors who must be given access to company secrets. The noncompetition contracts set out in Chapter 5 are designed to be used when you hire an employee; Form 905 assumes the "employee" actually will be an independent contractor. Do not assume that this agreement should be used only for high-level consultants. If, for example, you use a local person to keyboard and print your customer mailing list, that person may have complete access to your company's most precious asset.

Form 906 can be used to transfer title to virtually any type of personal property. It contains representations by the seller regarding good title and warranties by both parties that the sale was not made through the efforts of a broker. Both parties should protect themselves by having a third person witness the agreement or by having a notary public take their signatures.

Specialized Contract Forms

Forms 907 and 908 are similar to Form 404 (Lease Extension) in that they extend the time to complete the agreement. Form 907 should be used when the contract itself is being extended; Form 908 should be used when one party will be given more time to complete his or her end of the bargain.

Form 909 should be used when both parties agree to end an existing contractual relationship. The signing of this contract need not be witnessed (or notarized), but careful businesspeople generally will use a witness to ensure that the signing is not questioned at some later date.

Forms 910 through 913 offer different types of release formats. Although it is not required by law, it is certainly wise to have an independent third person (or a notary public) witness the signing of the release forms.

Forms 910 through 913 are releases of liens or claims by creditors. Form 910 is a general release in which one person releases the other from liability. It can be used for any type of liability regardless of the source of the liability. Form 911 is similar to Form 910, except that in this form both sides are releasing the other. Form 912 is a release in which one person releases only a specified portion of his or her claim against a second person. Form 913 can be used to issue a release of a mechanic's or materialman's lien against real property.

Corporate and Partnership Forms

Forms 914 and 915 are proxy forms designed to be used when one person has agreed to let another person vote the first person's shares of stock in a corporation. These forms can be used in conjunction with a loan, e.g., where the shares are pledged as collateral, or in conjunction with the sale of the shares after the record date and before a shareholders' meeting.

Neither of these forms should be used if the corporation's board of directors issues the proxy. In such cases, either federal or state law may govern the form of the proxy, and you should seek out your company's attorney before issuing such a proxy form. Form 914 is a simple, straightforward revocable proxy form. Under state law, it can be revoked at any time. The person granting the proxy need only attend the meeting and announce that he or she is revoking the proxy and will vote the shares himself or herself. Similarly, this form of proxy is deemed revoked if the person subsequently issues another proxy in favor of another person. Form 915 is irrevocable. This means the proxy may not be rescinded during the term noted on the proxy.

Form 916 should be given to a corporation when you have lost your share certificate. You will not be issued a replacement certificate without this notarized affidavit. If you have lost shares that were issued by a corporation whose shares are listed on a major stock exchange or are traded over the market, you may wish to call your stockbroker and request the form required by the corporation.

Form 917 can be used to create a partnership form of business. Once you and your partner have agreed on the amounts that each of you will invest in the business and how each of you will share in its profits, you have all the information you need to complete this form.

Powers of Attorney

Forms 918 and 919 are powers of attorney. Most people think of powers of attorney in the context of a tool that should be used when someone becomes incompetent. However, they also have their place in the small-business setting. If, for example, you operate a small business and expect to be absent because you will be taking that long-awaited extended vacation, you may have to delegate specific authority to a trusted individual to carry out certain functions for you. People accustomed to dealing directly with you may not be willing to deal with a subordinate in the absence of some form of written authorization.

Form 918 sets out a power of attorney for a limited purpose—you must describe the power you are granting precisely to ensure that your representative can do everything you wish him or her to do, but no more than that. Form 919 is a general, unlimited power of attorney. Both forms must be notarized.

Affidavits and Bulk Sales

Form 920 can be used whenever you must supply an affidavit for a statement that has to be made under oath. Forms 921 and 922 are required to comply with the Bulk Sales provisions of the UCC. A bulk sale is one that you would not make in the ordinary course of business. For example, if you operated a shop that offered duplicating services, you would not, as part of your ordinary business operations, sell your duplicating machines and your entire stock of toner and paper.

Forms 921 and 922 should be used only if your existing creditors will be paid from the proceeds of the sale. If your creditors will not be paid from the proceeds of the sale, you should consult with your attorney before going ahead with the sale.

Form 921 provides the affidavit required when a bulk sale is made and states that the seller owns the property in question free and clear of all liens. This form must be notarized. You can use Form 922 to provide the notice of the sale to your creditors. To comply with the UCC, you must give your creditors not less than ten (10) days notice of the scheduled sale date. Although not required by law, hand delivery (with an affidavit that delivery was made) or registered mail, return receipt requested, is the recommended form of service.

CONDITIONAL SALE AGREEMENT

AGREEMENT made this   day of   , 19   , by and between

(hereinafter "Seller") and

(hereinafter "Buyer").

Intending to be legally bound, the Buyer and the Seller agree as follows:

1. The Seller will sell to the Buyer and the Buyer will purchase the items listed on Schedule A.

2. The purchase price shall be:

    Price:

    Sales tax:

    Finance charges:

    Shipping charges:

    Total price:

3. The purchase price shall be paid with a down payment of   dollars ($) and the remaining amount in equal installments of   dollars ($), payable on the   day of the month.

4. This is a conditional sales agreement. Title will not pass to the Buyer until payment in full has been received by the Seller.

5. The Seller retains the right to repossess the items sold, subject to any apportionment for payments received, should the Buyer fail or refuse to make all necessary payments.

_____

Buyer

_____

Seller

THIS FORM MUST BE RECORDED WITH YOUR LOCAL FILING OFFICE OR IT WILL NOT BE EFFECTIVE AGAINST SUBSEQUENT LENDERS.

CONSIGNMENT AGREEMENT

THIS CONSIGNMENT AGREEMENT is made this   day of   , 19   ,

by and between   (hereinafter "Consignor") and

(hereinafter "Consignee").

The parties intending to be legally bound agree as follows:

1. The property delivered to the Consignee, as listed in the attached schedule, shall remain the property of the Consignor.

2. The Consignee will display the items delivered at its business location.

3. The Consignee will return on demand any property of the Consignor prior to its sale, and the Consignee promises to return said property in good and marketable condition.

4. The Consignee will use its best business efforts to sell said items on behalf of the Consignor, at a minimum price as established by the Consignor.

5. The Consignee will remit the proceeds of the sale to the Consignor within   (   ) days of sale, said funds to be segregated from the accounts of the Consignee.

6. The Consignee will permit and allow the Consignor to inspect and audit the books and records of the Consignee with respect to the property of the Consignor.

7. The Consignee will execute all reasonable documents necessary to protect and ensure that the title to the items remains with the Consignor.

                                    _____

                                    Consignee

                                    _____

                                    Consignor

THIS FORM MUST BE RECORDED WITH YOUR LOCAL FILING OFFICE OR IT WILL NOT BE EFFECTIVE AGAINST SUBSEQUENT LENDERS.

INDEMNIFICATION AGREEMENT

IN CONSIDERATION OF GOOD AND VALUABLE CONSIDERATION, by t

made this   day of   , 19   , between

(the "Seller") and

(the "Purchaser"), the parties hereby agree:

1. Indemnification. The Seller agrees to indemnify and hold the

    Purchaser harmless at all times against and in respect of all

    actions, claims, suits, settlements, proceedings, demands,

    assessments, judgments, losses, costs, damages, disbursements

    and expenses incident to, arising from or with respect to the

    following transaction:

2. Notice. The Purchaser shall notify the Seller within   (   )

    days after receipt by the Purchaser of any notice of any informa-

    tion referable to Paragraph 1 above. However, the omission to so

    notify the Seller shall not relieve the Seller of any obligation

    on account thereof, except to the extent that the Seller was preju-

    diced by the Purchaser's failure to provide such notice.

3. <u>Benefit</u>. This agreement shall be binding upon and inure to the benefit of the parties hereto and their legal representatives, successors and assigns.

4. <u>Interpretation</u>. This agreement shall be interpreted in accordance with the laws of the state of   .

5. <u>Invalid Provision</u>. In the event any provision of this agreement is held to be void, invalid or unenforceable in any respect, then the same shall not affect the remaining provisions hereof, which shall continue in full force and effect.

6. <u>Entire Agreement</u>. This agreement contains the entire understanding of the parties. It may not be changed orally. This agreement may be amended or modified only in writing and such writing must be executed by both parties hereto.

IN WITNESS WHEREOF, the parties have executed this agreement the day and year first above written.

_____
Purchaser

_____
Seller

(Notary Public)

SUBSCRIPTION TO CORPORATE STOCK

FOR VALUABLE CONSIDERATION RECEIVED, I agree to purchase   (   )

shares of the capital stock of   (hereinafter

"Corporation") at a price of   dollars ($)

per share for a total amount of   dollars

($).

I have been informed that the shares I am purchasing will have all of

the rights and privileges of all shares of the same class of stock. Fur-

thermore, I am aware that the shares I am purchasing equals   per-

cent (%) of all issued and outstanding stock of the same class and

       percent (%) of all of the issued and outstanding stock

of the corporation, regardless of class.

The purchase price will be paid to the Corporation on or before

       , 19   .

_____

Purchaser

Agreed to and accepted:

_____

For the Above-Mentioned Corporation

NONCOMPETITION AGREEMENT

FOR CONSIDERATION RECEIVED, this agreement made this   day of

          , 19   , by and between

(hereinafter referred to as the "Principal") and

                         (hereinafter referred to as the "Consult-

ant").

WHEREAS, the Principal desires to engage the services of the Consultant

to assist the Principal in the operation of its business, it is agreed as

follows:

1. Purpose. The Principal engages the Consultant to assist the Princi-

    pal in the operation of its business.

2. Term. This agreement shall commence on   , 19   , and

    shall terminate on   , 19   .

3. Disclosure of Information. The Consultant acknowledges that the

    list of the Principal's customers as it may exist from time to

    time is a valuable, special and unique asset of the Principal's

    business. The Consultant shall not, during or after the term of

    this agreement, disclose the list of the Principal's customers or

    any part thereof to any person, firm, corporation, association or

    other entity for any reason or purpose whatsoever. In the event of

    a breach or threatened breach by the Consultant of the provisions

    of this paragraph, the Principal shall be entitled to an injunc-

    tion restraining the Consultant from disclosing, in whole or in part, the list of the Principal's customers or from rendering any services to any person, firm, corporation, association or other entity to whom such list, in whole or in part, has been disclosed or is threatened to be disclosed. Nothing herein shall be construed as prohibiting the Principal from pursuing any other remedies available to the Principal for such breach or threatened breach, including the recovery of damages from the Consultant.

4. <u>Notices</u>. Any notice required or desired to be given under this agreement shall be deemed given if in writing sent by certified mail to his or her residence in the case of the Consultant or to its principal office in the case of the Principal.

5. <u>Assignment</u>. The Consultant acknowledges that the services to be rendered by him or her are unique and personal. Accordingly, the Consultant may not assign any of his or her rights or delegate any of his or her duties or obligations under this agreement. The rights and obligations of the Principal under this agreement shall inure to the benefit of and shall be binding upon the successors and assigns of the Principal.

6. <u>Status of Consultant</u>. The Consultant is engaged as an independent contractor and shall be treated as such for all purposes, including, but not limited to, federal and state taxation, withholding, unemployment insurance and worker's compensation. The Consultant will not be considered an employee for any purpose.

7. <u>Entire Agreement</u>. This agreement contains the entire understanding of the parties. It may not be changed orally but only by an agreement in writing signed by the party against whom enforcement of any waiver, change, modification, extension or discharge is sought.

IN WITNESS WHEREOF, the parties have executed this agreement the day and year first above written.

WITNESS:

_____

                                    _____

                                    Principal

                                    _____

                                    Consultant

PERSONAL PROPERTY SALES CONTRACT

AGREEMENT made this   day of   , 19   , between

                    (hereinafter "Seller") and

                    (hereinafter "Purchaser").

1. The Property. The Seller has agreed to sell and the Purchaser has

    agreed to buy the following personal property:

2. Purchase Price. The purchase price for the property described in

    paragraph 1 above shall be   dollars

    ($) and shall be paid as follows:

    (a)   dollars ($) upon the

        execution of this agreement and

    (b) The balance of   dollars ($)

        payable in   (   ) equal monthly installments with

        interest at the rate of   percent (%) per annum,

        the first payment to begin   (   ) days after the execu-

        tion of this agreement. This obligation shall be evidenced by

        a promissory note, a copy being attached hereto, made a part

        hereof and designated as "Exhibit A."

3. <u>Warranties of the Seller</u>. The Seller hereby warrants and represents to the Purchaser that:

   (a) The Seller owns and has good and marketable title to the property being conveyed herein, free and clear of any pledges, liens, judgments, encumbrances, security interests, claims or contract rights, and further promises and covenants to refrain from so encumbering same from the date of execution of this agreement until closing;

   (b) No approval or consent of any third person is required to effect the sale;

   (c) The execution and performance of this agreement will not violate any agreements to which the Seller is a party or any federal, state or local laws, rules or regulations;

   (d) The Seller's representations, warranties and agreements shall be true and complete as of the date hereof and as of the closing and shall survive the closing and the transactions contemplated by this agreement.

4. <u>Broker</u>. Both the Seller and the Purchaser warrant and represent that no broker was involved in negotiating this purchase and sale, and both the Seller and the Purchaser agree to indemnify and hold each other harmless against any and all claims for brokerage.

5. Benefit. This agreement shall be binding upon and inure to the benefit of the parties hereto and their legal representatives, successors and assigns.

6. Interpretation. This agreement shall be interpreted in accordance with the laws of the state of

7. Invalid Provision. In the event any provision or subprovision of this agreement is held to be void, invalid or unenforceable in any respect, then the same shall not affect the remaining provisions or subprovisions hereof, which shall continue in full force and effect.

8. Entire Agreement. This agreement contains the entire understanding of the parties. It may not be changed orally. This agreement may only be amended or modified in writing and with such writing being executed by both parties hereto.

IN WITNESS WHEREOF, the parties have executed this agreement the day and year first above written.

_____

Seller

_____

Purchaser

WITNESS:

_____

AGREEMENT EXTENDING A CONTRACT

FOR CONSIDERATION mutually exchanged between the parties,

                        and   , this

extension agreement is made this   day of   , 19   .

    WHEREAS,   and

have previously entered into an agreement dated   , 19   , and

    WHEREAS, said agreement will conclude on   , 19   , and

    WHEREAS, both parties desire to extend the above-mentioned agreement,

    NOW, therefore, intending to be legally bound, both parties agree as

follows:

    1. The agreement shall be lengthened for an additional term of

        .

    2. In all other respects, said agreement shall continue in full force

        and effect.

    IN WITNESS WHEREOF, the parties have executed this agreement the day

and year first above written.

                            _____

                            _____

WITNESS:

_____

PERFORMANCE EXTENSION

FOR CONSIDERATION mutually exchanged between the parties,

_____ and _____ , this per-

formance extension agreement is made this   day of   , 19   .

WHEREAS, _____ and

have previously entered into an agreement dated   , 19   , and

WHEREAS, said agreement requires performance on or before   ,

19   ,

WHEREAS, both parties desire to extend the agreement,

NOW, therefore intending to be legally bound, both parties agree as

follows:

1. The due date of performance shall be   , 19   .

2. In all other respects, said agreement shall continue in full force

    and effect.

IN WITNESS WHEREOF, the parties have executed this agreement the day

and year first above written.

_____

_____

WITNESS:

_____

CONTRACT TERMINATION

FOR CONSIDERATION mutually exchanged between the parties,

and   , this agree-

ment is made this   day of   , 19   .

WHEREAS,   and

have previously entered into an agreement dated   , 19   ; and

WHEREAS, both parties desire to terminate the agreement:

NOW, therefore intending to be legally bound, both parties agree as

follows:

   1.   The above-described agreement shall cease as of   ,

        19   .

   2.   Both parties agree to release each other of liability.

   3.   In all other respects, said agreement shall continue in full force

        and effect.

IN WITNESS WHEREOF, the parties have executed this agreement the day

and year first above written.

                              _____

                              _____

WITNESS:

_____

GENERAL RELEASE

Date:

IN CONSIDERATION of one dollar ($1) and other valuable consideration

received, I,   , relieve and release

                    (hereinafter "Obligor"), his or her heirs and

assigns from all claims and liabilities owed to me by the Obligor as of

the date of the execution of this release.

———————————————

(Notary Public)

MUTUAL RELEASE

Date:

IN CONSIDERATION of one dollar ($1), this mutual release and other valu-

able consideration received,   and

relieve, release and discharge each other,

their heirs and assigns from all claims and liabilities or obligations

whether flowing from contracts, lawsuits or any other source and that will

have arisen on or before the date of this release.

_____

_____

(Notary Public)

SPECIFIC RELEASE

IN CONSIDERATION of one dollar ($1) and other valuable consideration

received, I,   , relieve and release

                                        , his or her heirs and assigns from all claims

and liabilities arising out of the following:

This release shall not act as a release of any other debt or claim to

which I may have against   .

_____

(Notary Public)

LIEN RELEASE

IN CONSIDERATION of one dollar ($1) and other valuable consideration re-

ceived, I, _____ , relieve and release

_____ from all mechanics, materialman or labor

liens that I have filed, before the date set out below, against the real

property located at:

Date: _____

_____

(Notary Public)

REVOCABLE PROXY

FOR AND IN CONSIDERATION of one dollar ($1) and other valuable considera-
tion, I hereby bestow on _____ a proxy to vote on
my behalf   (   ) shares of _____ (hereinafter
"Corporation") at the shareholders' meeting to be held on _____ ,
19   , and all subsequent regular and special meetings of shareholders of
the Corporation.

The holder of this proxy shall have all the rights and privileges to
vote and attend meetings as I do. Until this proxy is revoked, I shall not
act to vote the shares represented by this proxy. This proxy is revocable
without notice.

Date: _____

_____

IRREVOCABLE PROXY

FOR AND IN CONSIDERATION of one dollar ($1), I hereby bestow on

a proxy to vote on my behalf

(   ) shares of stock of   (hereinafter

"Company") at the shareholders' meeting to be held on   , 19   .

   The holder of this proxy shall have all the rights and privileges to

vote and attend the aforesaid meeting as I do. This proxy, which may not

be revoked by me, shall not extend beyond the shareholders' meeting, or

any extension thereof, to be held on   , 19   .

Date: _____

_____

AFFIDAVIT: LOST STOCK CERTIFICATE

State of   :

County of   :

I,   , residing at

                            , being duly sworn, depose:

1. I am the owner of   (   ) shares of

    (hereinafter "Company"), represented by share certificate number

    .

2. That I have lost or mislaid said share certificate.

3. That I have not sold or transferred said certificate.

4. That I agree to indemnify the Company for any loss as a result of

    a claim by any holder in due course of the said lost certificate.

    _____

Sworn to before me on   , 19   .

(Notary Public)

PARTNERSHIP AGREEMENT

THIS AGREEMENT made this   day of   , 19   , by and among

                              (hereinafter referred to as "Partner One")

and   (hereinafter referred to as "Partner

Two").

WHEREAS, Partner One and Partner Two desire to form a partnership in

the state of   .

NOW, THEREFORE, in consideration of the mutual covenants and agreements

contained herein, the parties hereto, intending to be legally bound

hereby, agree as follows:

1. The parties hereby form a partnership that will engage in the busi-

    ness of   under the name of

                    .

2. The partners ownership interest and capital account shall be as

    follows:

3. The principal office of the partnership is to be located at

                              , or in such other place as the

    parties may agree.

4. The partnership shall exist for a period of   , commencing

   on   , 19   , and shall continue until   ,

   19   , unless terminated earlier as hereinafter provided.

5. Either party to this partnership agreement may withdraw from the

   partnership upon six (6) months notice to the remaining party to

   this partnership agreement.

6. The partners shall share the profits and losses of the partnership

   in relationship to their ownership interest.

7. This partnership agreement shall immediately terminate upon the

   death of either partner.

8. All controversies arising under or in connection with, or relating

   to any alleged breach of, this partnership agreement shall be set-

   tled by arbitration in accordance with the rules then obtaining of

   the American Arbitration Association, and judgment upon any award

   rendered may be entered in any court having jurisdiction.

9. This partnership agreement shall be binding upon and inure to the

   benefit of the parties hereto and their respective heirs, execu-

   tors, administrators, successors and assigns.

10. This partnership agreement constitutes the entire agreement be-

    tween the parties hereto and supersedes all prior agreements,

    negotiations and understandings of any nature with respect to the

    subject matter hereto. No amendment, waiver or discharge of any of

the provisions of this agreement shall be effective against any party unless that party shall have consented thereto in writing.

11. This partnership agreement shall be construed, interpreted and enforced in accordance with the laws of the state of   .

IN WITNESS WHEREOF, Partner One and Partner Two have caused this partnership agreement to be duly executed the day and year set out above.

IN WITNESS WHEREOF, the parties have executed this agreement the day and year first above written.

_____

_____

WITNESS: _____

LIMITED POWER OF ATTORNEY

KNOW ALL PERSONS BY THESE PRESENTS, that I,   ,

residing at   , do hereby make, constitute and

appoint   , residing at

                              , as the true and lawful attorney-in-fact

for me and in my name, place and stead, and on my behalf, and for my use

and benefit with respect to the following matter(s):

This instrument shall be construed and interpreted as a limited power

of attorney.

The enumeration of specific items, rights or powers herein shall not

limit or restrict, and is not to be construed or interpreted as limiting

or restricting, the limited powers herein granted to said attorney-in-

fact.

The rights, powers and authority of said attorney-in-fact granted in

this instrument shall commence and be in full force and effect on

                , 19   , and such rights, powers and authority shall remain

in full force and effect thereafter until I,   ,

give notice in writing that such power is terminated.

It is my desire, and I so freely state, that this power of attorney shall not be affected by my subsequent disability or incapacity. Furthermore, upon a finding of incompetence by a court of appropriate jurisdiction, this power of attorney shall be irrevocable until such time as said court determines that I am no longer incompetent.

_____

I, _____, whose name is signed to the foregoing instrument, having been duly qualified according to the law, do hereby acknowledge that I signed and executed this power of attorney; that I am of sound mind; that I am eighteen (18) years of age or older; that I signed it willingly and am under no constraint or undue influence; and that I signed it as my free and voluntary act for the purpose therein expressed.

_____

(Notary Public)

FULL POWER OF ATTORNEY

Date:

KNOW ALL PERSONS BY THESE PRESENTS, that I,   ,

residing at   , do hereby make, constitute and

appoint   , residing at

                                   , as the true and lawful attorney-in-fact

for me and in my name, place and stead, and on my behalf, and for my use

and benefit, in the following matters:

1. To ask, demand, sue for, recover and receive all manner of goods,

    chattels, debts, rents, interest, sums of money and demands whatso-

    ever, due or hereafter to become due and owing, or belonging to

    me, and to make, give and execute acquittances, receipts, satisfac-

    tions or other discharges for the same, whether under seal or oth-

    erwise;

2. To make, execute, endorse, accept and deliver in my name or in the

    name of my aforesaid attorney all checks, notes, drafts, warrants,

    acknowledgments, agreements and all other instruments in writing,

    of whatever nature, as to my said attorney-in-fact may seem neces-

    sary to conserve my interests;

3. To execute, acknowledge and deliver any and all contracts, debts,

    leases, assignments of mortgage, extensions of mortgage, satisfac-

    tions of mortgage, releases of mortgage, subordination agreements

    and any other instrument or agreement of any kind or nature

whatsoever, in connection therewith, and affecting any and all property presently mine or hereafter acquired, located anywhere, which to my said attorney-in-fact may seem necessary or advantageous for my interests;

4. To enter into and take possession of any lands, real estate, tenements, houses, stores or buildings, or parts thereof, belonging to me that may become vacant or unoccupied, or to the possession of which I may be or may become entitled, and to receive and take for me and in my name and to my use all or any rents, profits or issues of any real estate to me belonging, and to let the same in such manner as to my attorney shall seem necessary and proper, and from time to time to renew leases;

5. To commence, and prosecute in my behalf, any suits or actions or other legal or equitable proceedings for the recovery of any of my lands or for any goods, chattels, debts, duties, demand, cause or thing whatsoever, due or to become due or belonging to me, and to prosecute, maintain and discontinue the same, if he or she shall deem proper;

6. To take all steps and remedies necessary and proper for the conduct and management of my business affairs, and for the recovery, receiving, obtaining and holding possession of any lands, tenements, rents or real estate, goods and chattels, debts, interest, demands, duties, sum or sums of money or any other thing

whatsoever, located anywhere, that is, are or shall be, by my said attorney-in-fact, thought to be due, owing, belonging to or payable to me in my own right or otherwise;

7. To appear, answer and defend in all actions and suits whatsoever that shall be commenced against me and also for me and in my name to compromise, settle and adjust, with each and every person or persons, all actions, accounts, dues and demands, subsisting or to subsist between me and them or any of them, and in such manner as my said attorney-in-fact shall think proper; hereby giving to my said attorney power and authority to do, execute and perform and finish for me and in my name all those things that shall be expedient and necessary, or which my said attorney shall judge expedient and necessary in and about or concerning the premises, or any of them, as fully as I could do if personally present, hereby ratifying and confirming whatever my said attorney shall do or cause to be done in, about or concerning the premises and any part thereof.

This instrument shall be construed and interpreted as a general power of attorney.

The enumeration of specific items, rights or powers herein shall not limit or restrict, and is not to be construed or interpreted as limiting or restricting, the general powers herein granted to said attorney-in-fact.

The rights, powers and authority of said attorney-in-fact granted in this instrument shall commence and be in full force and effect on

, 19   , and such rights, powers and authority shall remain in full force and effect thereafter until I give notice in writing that such power is terminated.

It is my desire, and I so freely state, that this power of attorney shall not be affected by my subsequent disability or incapacity. Furthermore, upon a finding of incompetence by a court of appropriate jurisdiction, this power of attorney shall be irrevocable until such time as said court determines that I am no longer incompetent.

_____

I,   , whose name is signed to the foregoing instrument, having been duly qualified according to the law, do hereby acknowledge that I signed and executed this power of attorney; that I am of sound mind; that I am eighteen (18) years of age or older; that I signed it willingly and am under no constraint or undue influence; and that I signed it as my free and voluntary act for the purpose therein expressed.

_____

(*Notary Public*)

AFFIDAVIT

State of   :

County of   :

I,   , residing at

                  , being duly sworn, deposes and swears:

This affidavit is made for the purpose of:

_____

Sworn to before me on   , 19   .

(Notary Public)

BULK SALES AFFIDAVIT

State of   :

County of   :

The undersigned,   , residing at

                    , being duly sworn, deposes:

1. I am the   President and sole shareholder of

    the business known as   (hereinafter

    "Corporation") and I am the person who executed the annexed bill

    of sale on behalf of the Corporation.

2. The Corporation is the sole owner of the property described in the

    foregoing bill of sale, and it has the full right to sell and

    transfer this property.

3. All of the property described in the foregoing bill of sale is

    free and clear of all obligations and encumbrances.

4. There are no judgments existing against the Corporation in any

    court; nor are there any replevins, liens, attachments or execu-

    tions issued against the Corporation; nor has any petition in bank-

    ruptcy nor any arrangement proceeding been filed by or against the

    Corporation; nor has the Corporation taken advantage of any law re-

    lating to insolvency.

This affidavit is made to induce   (here-

inafter "Buyer") to accept the transfer of the property described in the foregoing bill of sale and to pay consideration therefor. It also is made to assure compliance with the bulk transfer provisions of the Uniform Commercial Code as it is in force in the state of   and to assure that there are no creditors of the Corporation who are entitled to the statutory notice of sale.

———————————————

(Notary Public)

NOTICE TO CREDITORS UNDER THE BULK SALES ACT

To: The Creditors of   Corporation:

On   , 19   ,   (hereinafter the

"Seller") intends to transfer all of its goods listed herein

                      which are located at

              to

(hereinafter "Buyer") in what shall be a bulk sale for new consideration

of   dollars ($).

   To the best of the Buyer's knowledge, the Seller has not transacted

business under a different name during the past three years. The Seller's

outstanding debts will be satisfied in full pursuant to this bulk sale.

   You, as a creditor, are to send your bills to:

   This notice is provided to conform to the requirements of Article 6 of

the Uniform Commercial Code.

   The total debts of the Seller are   dollars

($).

                  Sincerely,

                  _____

Index

About the Author

Ted Nicholas is a multifaceted business personality. In addition to being a well-known author and respected speaker, Mr. Nicholas remains an active participant in his own entrepreneurial ventures. Without capital, he started his first business at age 21. Since then, he has started 22 companies of his own.

Mr. Nicholas has written 13 books on business and finance since his writing career began in 1972. The best known is *How To Form Your Own Corporation Without a Lawyer for under $75.* His previous business enterprises include Peterson's House of Fudge, a candy and ice cream manufacturing business conducted through 30 retail stores, as well as other businesses in franchising, real estate, machinery and food.

When the author was only 29, he was selected by a group of business leaders as one of the most outstanding businessmen in the nation and was invited to the White House to meet the President.

Although Mr. Nicholas has founded many successful enterprises, he also has experienced two major setbacks and many minor ones. He considers business setbacks necessary to success and the only true way to learn anything in life, a lesson that goes all the way back to childhood. That's why he teaches other entrepreneurs how to "fail forward."

Mr. Nicholas has appeared on numerous television and radio shows and conducts business seminars in Florida and Switzerland. Presently, he owns and operates four corporations of his own and acts as marketing consultant and copywriter to small as well as large businesses.

If you have any questions, thoughts or comments, Mr. Nicholas loves to hear from his readers! You are welcome to call, write or fax him at the following address:

Nicholas Direct, Inc.
19918 Gulf Boulevard, #7
Indian Shores, FL 34635
Phone: 813-596-4966
Fax: 813-596-6900